MILITIA JUSTICE

THE FALL OF A WRESTLING LEGEND

LANDON PARKER

Fulton Books
Meadville, PA

Published by Fulton Books 2022

This is a work of nonfiction. Some names have been changed, but the book is based on true events.

ISBN 978-1-63985-673-2 (paperback)
ISBN 978-1-63985-674-9 (digital)

Printed in the United States of America

To my mother, Dr. Peggy J. Parker
I miss you every moment of every second.
Thank you for being my real-life hero.

I'll be seeing you in all the old familiar places.
That this heart of mine embraces all day through,
In the small café and the park across the way,
At the children's carousel, chestnut tree, and the wishing well,
I'll be seeing you in every lovely summer's day,
I'll always think of you that way,
I'll find you in the morning sun,
And when the night is new, I'll be looking at the moon.
But I'll be seeing you.

*****

Blessed is the man who perseveres under trial because
when he has stood the test, he shall receive the crown of
life that God has promised to those who love him.

—James 1:12

CONTENTS

PROLOGUE

T he year is 1968, and the residents of Evanston, Illinois, were just entering the end of February. Faint sunlight faded into billowing cumulus clouds that now swept over the building tops of Northwestern University. At the same time, just north of Ryan field, snowflakes fell on the shoulders of rows of the people now milling into McGaw Hall to watch their sons, brothers, and loved ones compete in the High School State Championships. McGaw Memorial Hall is known for being the third largest arena in the Midwest. Today, this historic arena is home to the tournament of champions where warriors collide and heroes are born. Vibrant and chiseled, seventeen-year-old Phil Parker paced the locker room's annals, preparing mentally for his chance to win the 127-pound state championship title. The overhead lights glimmered against his bronze skin tone as the handsome, stocky, African American youth trudged the dark, quiet edifice. Shadowing his path were his older brother, Charles, and his eldest brother, Sam.

Sam Parker's no stranger to the emotions of a championship competitor. This was the place where, in 1964, Sam had earned his own 127-pound state championship crown. Phil kept a red-and-gold North Chicago War Hawk hooded sweatshirt draped over his head while carefully plotting his plan of attack in the shadows. Charles and Sam were proudly wearing blue jeans with brand-new, white, long-sleeved dress shirts.

"Phil, keep wrestling like a warrior out there. You deserve to wear a robe today, champ," Charles said.

Phil admired Charles for being the most dapper, regal, and strongly proportioned of all his brothers. Few could imagine the physical and spiritual realms Phil had cleared to get to this pivotal moment in his wrestling career.

"It's time to consummate the victories. I need to win. Everything's on the line here," Phil replied, leading his older brothers through McGaw Hall and back into the gymnasium.

"This is your chance. Don't blow it! Don't let yourself down!" Sam said, folding his arms over his chest. Sam Parker was swarthy, broad shouldered, and built like a tank.

"In the whole scope of things, this match is one to remember. Victory is your light at the end of the tunnel. Hold on to it, Phil. Don't ever let go," Charles interjected as they continued through the noisy and crowded arena.

"Thanks for your support, family," Phil grunted, taking in the scent of blood, sweat, and tears before parting ways with his two older brothers to join the other finalists on the center mat.

Seconds later, all 180 overhead mercury lights dimmed, and the champions of champions were now standing face-to-face with the best of the best. Phil was staring blankly ahead, thinking about the lives lost to racism and civil injustice. He closed his eyes, imagining Emmet Till and Medgar Evers, and quickly realized that this was a golden opportunity to claim his place in the Civil Rights Movement. Phil was eyeing the short, blond Max Branum of Rich East High; his only loss the year before, the returning state champion, and the only high school wrestler of their decade who hadn't lost a match in his career. It was North versus East, black versus white, and champion versus champion.

The entire gym went pitch-black until the spotlight went streaking through the darkness, beaming on the last mat left unrolled in the building. Phil stood in place across from Max Branum, feeling the nerves raging within, and when they called his name, he hurried to meet Branum at the center of the mat. The two exceptional young men shook hands in the light. As their palms touched, Phil looked into Branum's deep blue eyes, checking for fear or uncertainty, and was perhaps overwhelmed by the moment Branum broke the gaze.

Sensing fear, Phil went back into the huddle of warriors, now with more confidence than ever before. The two studs took opposite sides of the mat with a mix of adrenaline and fire rushing through their veins. Forty minutes later, a hush went through the crowd as Parker and Branum posed in wrestling stances on opposite sides of the circle with muscles tensing. The crowd moved to the edges of their seats, waiting for the tournament's most anticipated battle to commence. Within seconds, the whistle blew, and the action began. They fought hands for what seemed an eternity, and by the end of the first period, the match remained scoreless.

By the beginning of the second period, both wrestlers were panting for breath. Branum fell into the referee's position, and Phil affirmed his place on top, waiting for the referee to blow the whistle. Although they were both tossing and fighting for position, Phil rode Branum the entire period. At the beginning of the third and final period, Phil chose the down and assumed the referee's position, looking like a madman. He dripped with sweat and staring blankly ahead, noticed his parents watching from the stands. When the whistle blew, Phil shot to his feet and broke free. In response to the action, the referee lifted his arm and raised a finger crediting Phil one point. The scoreboard read one-zero as Phil battled on in what was to be the most important match of his life.

Phil then hit Branum with sweeping a double leg from somewhere far outside the circle. Branum scrambled for the dominant position, locking his hands in between Phil's legs, and preparing for the Granby roll. Phil, being privy to most of Branum's signature moves, left his embattled opponent suspended in the air until the referee broke the action. The two wrestlers warred down to the last few ticks of the time clock, and by the end of the match, Parker had captured the 127-pound State Championship. A tremendous sensation surged through his entire body as his hand was raised before a crowd of thousands. Completely exhausted, Phil fell to his back, looked up to the ceiling, and quietly thanked God. And from this moment on, the road of his life would continue to become shinier and brighter. His parents and siblings were parading in the stands, and when Phil arose, his coach, Bob Terry, was nowhere to be found.

Later that evening, Coach Terry resurfaced to drape the first-place medal around Phil's neck.

During the exchange, the old man said in a low tone, "Son, you could beat Superman."

Phil went on to win the High School National Championship, becoming the most outstanding wrestler in the nation. During the National Tournament, he attracted the attention of legendary Iowa State Wrestling coach Harold "Nick" Nichols. Nick offered Phil a full-ride scholarship to join the elite Cyclone Alumni, and thus, the journey of a sports icon began. Phil left the rough, crime-infested streets of the Windy City behind, determined to take on a new mission. His goal was to be the greatest wrestler ever, and it would be no small feat to outshine the accomplishments of his eight other brothers, all of whom were wrestlers owning their sense of history on the wrestling mat. Generations would follow in his footsteps as more imprints in the sands of time, plotting the same journeys led by Phil's shining star. Phil's light continues to lead the charge of our family legacy. Here is the story of Phil Parker, our dearest champion, our North Chicago star.

CHAPTER 1

Destinies Begin

It all began one crisp fall morning, November 1, 1978, when Margaret Jean Phelan gave birth to her firstborn son, Landon Anthony Parker. Just hours before the traumatic birth, she later recalled walking the pale sand of the beach, watching the tide roll in, oblivious to the fact that her water was breaking. At that moment, while staring into the endless sea, her unborn son resting in her belly, she felt ready to take on the world. Born only six pounds and seven ounces, Landon Anthony Parker entered this world before his mother's and father's very eyes. Phil Parker, the current Ventura College head wrestling coach, planned his son's future while watching his newborn turn and toss in the incubator. Phil's career took off when he claimed both the state and national titles and, in turn, cemented his legacy as a War Hawk legend. He was already a champion long before deciding to accept Nick's full-ride scholarship to wrestle for the Iowa Cyclones. After four years of competing alongside Olympians Dan Gable, Ben Peterson, and Chris Taylor, Phil was steadily paving his way to the pinnacle of his career.

Phil was working as a campus cop and acting as the head coach of the Ventura Junior College Wrestling Team as a means to pay for his master's degree in counseling. Peggy and Phil lived in the Ventura villages long enough for both of them to earn master's degrees. Then in 1979, Phil was offered the job to be head wrestling coach of the Washington State Cougars. With that, the three of us soon left California. Determined to see our dreams come true, we set our sights on Pullman, Washington—the place we would soon call home.

To the college town of Pullman, Phil Parker was known as the young, fresh, big-shot head wrestling coach that everyone seemed to know; although, from my perspective, he was just Daddy. I adored the way the sun would shine by midafternoons on the hillsides, and how the smell of fresh rhubarb would hit the air every time I opened the sliding glass doors of the sunroom. Life seemed so simple during those sweet, careless, youthful days. Time flowed by like the cool winter breeze, and I was proud to be the coach's son. Everyone knew that we weren't like everyone else. We were real, certified champions. "Superman All the Time" was the philosophy we followed. It must have been trips to Snake River and times spent sipping cider throughout those cold November nights that made us learn to love those Washington apples with such a passion. We owned a beautiful, Victorian-style, three-storied home nestled almost at the end of State Street, and that was the home I would always favor from the rest.

Ann Parker was born seven pounds, three ounces on September 19, 1980, in Moscow, Idaho. Now, there were four of us. Ann was a quiet baby who smiled and laughed most of the time. With this beautiful new addition, my family was happy to make Pullman, Washington, ours. Dad was always at the University of Washington, working, coaching, and exercising; and Mom, when not at home with us, was busy rushing through WSU hallways pursuing a doctorate in psychology. We soon became accustomed the slow pace of this georgic, Bruce Springsteen-type small town. The mood of our city was electric when they built the first local youth recreation center just a few blocks away from Washington State University. The years blended to form a collage of my fondest memories. Dad gained popularity as he gradually rebuilt the wrestling program through active recruiting and yearly wrestling camps, and everywhere he went, he was always preaching his "Superman All the Time" philosophy, which began to shape the foundation of my technique. I don't think my father was ever into comic books, yet he was obsessed with Superman's mere idea. He felt that we, as athletes, should aspire to be superhuman out on the field of competition. Phil admired Superman and abhorred his alter ego, Clark Kent. He taught us never to settle and never to take our capes off. After school, I would sink onto the cushions of our rose-tinted love seat, waiting for Dad to come home, and sometimes he would cruise in the driveway behind the wheel of a brand-new Cougar sedan.

Michael Jackson had just shocked the world with his new album, *Thriller*, while Quincy Jones, Jeffery Osborne, and Billy Idol were rocking the airwaves on *MTV*, and Cindy Lauper was dropping her epic song, "Girls Just Want to Have Fun." Then, out of nowhere, the athletic director Dick Young dropped the wrestling program, and our sweet, precious, beautiful mom had to be rushed to the hospital. It was a crushing blow to our family structure when we learned of Momma's Crohn's disease diagnosis. However, she restored our hope by returning home, determined to make the most of her time left on this earth.

Our house, our garden, and our friends, we would all have to leave behind. Within weeks, Dad had accepted a job offer to be the head coach of Michigan State University's wrestling team. He would be the first and only African American coach in the school's history and also the first to coach in the Big Ten. And so we said goodbye to Washington's green hills and rolling pastures to begin our journey by automobile to East Lansing, Michigan.

On the way to Michigan, I watched mountains fade into the distance while counting the abandoned farmhouses; I was awestruck when I first laid eyes on those tree-lined avenues, exuding Spartan pride from block to block. East Lansing was a splendid change for us, and I was excited about making new friends. It felt like a great way to start off with a clean slate, and the mystery of not knowing the future intrigued me. I was seeking a fresh start in this cozy little college town. We seemed to be safe from the wild lifestyle of Lansing, but at that time, just a few miles away, on the Westside of town, gang activity was at an all-time high. I admired the Westside for that: everyone longs to be cool, and to a young kid, I guess that no one looked rougher than the real, certified *G*s. Staying cool is one of the most essential things of all, or at least it was for this mixed-up kid.

Michigan helped me forget how much I missed living in Washington. Our lovely home was located in the heart of a family-oriented, middle-class environment, just blocks away from Michigan State University. East Lansing is where we were to build a future, where we were to continue a legacy. Sparty was one of the first statues I remember admiring on our initial trip to the college campus. Standing tall and proud, his luminescent shadow cast its chiseled Romanesque silhouette against the walls of the Michigan State buildings. From my perspective, Sparty represented generations of scholarly achievements and the excellence that the university sought to produce. Fluttering gardens, ponds filled with swimming tadpoles, dancing in perfect synchronization, and lakes flourishing with ducks and swans were among the many attractions that made us fall in love with our new home in East Lansing, Michigan. Nothing was going to stop us now because we had pure love on our side, or so we thought.

◆ ◆ ◆ ◆ ◆

Michigan Dreams

We lived in an austere and handsome house on Milford Street, painted in a light-blue and cream tint, flaunting four yellow awnings over the front windows. This charming, vine-shaded home had served as the longtime ambassador of Milford Street. Some of my dearest moments were spent in the basement talking to Dad. And he would usually have something insightful to say. I hung on to his words every time he spoke about the epic battles that transpired in the Iowa State wrestling room. He rarely blinked when reminiscing about the arduous practices spent warring, bleeding, sweating, and crying. I asked him about Dan Gable, Ben Peterson, Chris Taylor, and Carl Adams, and indeed he told a story for them all. It seemed as if he had faced them at one point, and in the sport of wrestling, once you have met the best, then it's over. After that, there's no more speculation, no more false predictions. Only the champions went home with the bracket. I was almost twelve, and inspiration was everywhere I turned. The motivation was always prevalent in our home.

Still, beyond our seemingly perfect lives, voices whispered, "Did you see who he's married to?" Momma would later reflect. And most of the time, she would just laugh it off. It was pure bliss to be living those Michigan dreams, not knowing the hate was always looming. My mom was already a fantastic psychologist. I often observed her in action, implementing her favorite psychological techniques to pull through those awkward moments when the pain was unbearable. She seemed never to let it break her spirit. I admired Peggy J. Parker for all she was—the psychologist, the flying fistula woman, and the greatest mom in the world. Dad broke wrestling down to a science. Phil Parker was the best of the best, looking to prove to the world that his name belonged amongst the legends. The sport of wrestling was his life, and coaching was his passion. It was always a source of pride to be the son of the head wrestling coach of the Michigan State Spartans. It seemed like everyone knew Phil Parker, and most of the time they treated us like stars.

A kid's life was supposed to be free of the worries of adulthood, and mine was all the same, until one fateful night when we lost it all in an instant. My memory of that fateful Valentine's Day was a casual visit to the Loading Dock restaurant, where I fell deeply in love with my very first albacore tuna melt. Later that night, my father snuck out of the back door. And while I slept, a chance encounter would change our lives forever.

Twenty years later, I was sitting at the beige sectional couch in my parents' living room, looking to uncover the truth. I opened my pad, pulled the black ink pen away from the breast pocket of my light-blue dress shirt, and cleared my throat loud enough for my father to hear it. I intended to steer his attention away from the Lakers basketball game, which was edging into halftime, and my subtle gestures were no longer having the desired effect.

"So, Dad, tell me what happened?"

"What happened?"

"I want to write about it. I want to tell your story. Tell me what happened back at Michigan State University."

"Well, Landon, Dan Severn was out to get me from the start. I knew the minute I hired him that he wanted to take my place, and I foolishly gave him the opportunity. And you know why I did it?"

"No, why?"

"Bobby Douglas referred him to me."

"Bobby knew he was a racist?"

"His wife told me years later. See, Landon, it was a trap—it was a web of conspiracy that started with Dan. And he didn't act alone."

"Whom was he working with?"

"Grady."

"The former head coach, Grady Peninger?"

"Son, he's part of the good-ole-boy system, and he couldn't stand to see a Black man filling his shoes in the Michigan State wrestling room."

"So how do they relate to Jane Snow?"

"It's getting late. Let's finish this conversation tomorrow. You're welcome to stay the night."

"Yeah, I will."

Dad looked down, and for a moment, his eyes went distant and glossy. It seemed as if he wanted to tell me something but was holding back. I didn't want to press him any further. But deep down, I knew that he would talk when he was ready. And at that moment, I realized a part of him was still trapped somewhere in the fight to clear his name.

"Well, Landon, I'm about to call it a night," he grunted, rising to his full height. He then ran his fingertips across the white lettering of his favorite T-shirt. "Superman all the time," he whispered while reading the words on his shirt.

"That's the inside trip edition," I replied, touching the two white figures under the diamond-shaped emblem.

"I can't forget when you used the inside trip on the Arizona State champ. You owned that moment. You showed heart that night," he recalled.

"No one can ever take that away from me," I said with a smile.

"When I spoke to Grandma for the last time, she told me something. She told me to tell my story. She told me to tell it on the mountain, and then she began singing. 'Go, tell it on the mountain! Go, tell it on the mountain.' It's time, Landon."

"Thanks, Dad. We'll tell the story. We will do this together," I avowed, watching him walk out of the room.

I felt uneasy about our talk and was wrestling with the facts. Who was Jane Snow? Did they meet in a chance encounter, or did someone hire her? And where did Dan Severn fit into the equation? I found myself staring at the television but wasn't even watching anymore. Staring blankly ahead, I realized that a part of me was still there, in East Lansing, Michigan, where it all began. I took off my brown Dearfoams slippers and eased back on the king-sized bed in the guest room before surrendering to those sweet Michigan dreams. And the next thing I knew, it was August of 1990, and I was staring out of the window of a late model, midnight-black Nissan Sentra, watching a group of children gathering around, rushing water spewing from a broken fire hydrant on the corner. Red, yellow, and apple-green leaves were rustling through the breeze while Ann's doing her homework. Teddy Riley was singing "Don't Be Afraid" the rest of the way, and Dad was dancing as if no one was watching. I was always beaming with pride on those rare days when he would drive us to school.

All of my friends and classmates admired and respected Coach Parker. I was oblivious to his enemies, perhaps because he was kind to everyone. He treated his athletes as if they were his sons, and they loved him like a father. I anxiously stepped out of the car, threw my red backpack straps over my shoulder, and then went marching into the school grounds. Ann trailed my path until we eventually went our separate ways. When I reached my first class, I quickly found a seat in the back corner of the room. It was just another day at Hannah Middle School. Time was flying, and before I even knew it, the lunch bell rang, releasing us from boring lectures and quiet, awkward classrooms.

The eight of us met in the middle of the soccer field, ready as ever to release our pent-up energy and maybe earn some kudos from the girls milling close. Marcus began circling us, meticulously picking his team. Marcus Paxt, an awkward, skinny, dark-skinned African American transfer student from Central Michigan, was sizing us up. He had this chip on his shoulder because kids would tease him about his big ears and buckteeth.

"Who made you the captain?" I asked, resting my hands on my hips.

"I'm holding the pigskin, so that makes me the captain!" he shot back.

I didn't feel like arguing the point further, so I outstretched my arms and turned away.

"Just pick your team, and the remaining four are playing with me then," I said over my shoulder.

"Ross, Fred, and Kevin are on my team," he announced, throwing the football to Ross Smith.

Ross was tall and broad shouldered. His brown hair, bushy eyebrows, and a cocky smile that seldom fades made him appear arrogant to most. Fred Dawler was short and stocky. He had bright thatches of hair sprouting out of his black baseball cap, and his skin was ruddy and freckled. Kevin Zwad's family had recently moved here from Pakistan. He had dark hair and thick soda-bottle glasses. He was an average-sized kid, but he had the heart of a lion.

"Cool then Joe, Jeff, and Andy are on my team," I asserted, assembling my fellow ruffians, secretly hoping that they would be enough to lead me to uncertain victory.

Andy Green was dark-skinned and skinny. His shadow fade had three lines on the right side, and he was wearing long frayed jeans shorts. Joe and Jeff, the identical twins, were some of the most arrogant kids at school. They seemed to constantly be patting their greasy red hair and blowing kisses at the prettiest girls in school.

"What about me?" Ben asked, his voice seething with anxiety.

We all grunted under our breath being that Ben was the chubbiest, slowest, and dorkiest kid on this side of East Lansing. At that moment, I felt sorry for Ben, who stood there with his wavy, blond hair just swaying in the breeze. Wearing a yellow T-shirt stained with fresh ketchup stains, he had a look on his face like a part of him wanted to run in the other direction. Every day, Ben wore the same pair of black Levi's, and there was always a foul order resonating from somewhere on his person. He always seemed desperate to escape his tarnished reputation. I tried not to look him in those squinty, green eyes while humbly inviting him into my team.

"Okay, Ben, you can play on our side," I grunted, secretly saying goodbye to our chances at victory.

"Well, that's not fair. That would be five on four," Marcus complained. He was fuming as he stood there, throwing punches in the wind.

Brandon Pitts suddenly cut into the commotion. He was the tallest kid in the fifth grade, and he looked even more elevated in the brand-new black sweatpants he was wearing. None of the other kids wanted to contend with him, and he knew it. Brandon always sported a fresh flattop that was crisply bald faded.

"Don't even trip, Marcus, I'll join your team," Brandon said, stretching out his arms.

"Okay," Marcus grunted.

We took our opposite sides of the field.

"Let's crush those fools," I mumbled, calling my team into battle while Marcus hurled the pigskin toward us.

We all watched in confusion while the spinning ball dropped right into the hands of Ben Keen. Snarling, Keen cradled the pigskin and began tearing into enemy territory as if his life depended on it. He ran fearlessly, and for a moment, we didn't even recognize him. He was quick, agile, and nearly unstoppable.

Then we were all brought back to reality when Brandon steamrolled Ben before our very eyes and laid him out a few yards from our touchdown zone.

"Yes!" I yelled, rushing to my fallen teammate. "Good stuff, Ben. Hey, are you okay, man?" I inquired, standing over the fallen Keen.

The kid was gasping for breath, and just when I thought Ben's football days were over, he stood up.

"Let's show these punks how we do it," he whispered in a low tone, shocking us all with his bold new attitude.

"Okay. That's the spirit. Let's score the TD right now for my man, Ben," I announced, taking the ball out of Ben's hands.

"Let me play QB, Landon. I can throw it," Andy begged.

"Okay, man. Just make sure you make the play," I said, handing Andy the ball.

"On two, let's run one in for the cool kids," Andy said before setting the pigskin tip against the earth. "Hut one, hut two!" Andy's short, round face reddened as he yelled out the call, sending us running toward the various defenders.

Marcus was the first to break formation, and by that point, he was out for blood. Andy bobbed and weaved across the field, and by the look on his face, I knew he was becoming more and more desperate. And just when Marcus was about to lay him out like a pancake on the griddle, he threw the ball into the air, screaming.

The pigskin whirled into the breeze and then came down right into my grasp. I ran as fast as I could, right into the end zone. I was doing my best version of the celebration shuffle when the bell rang, sending us all back to class.

"That was smooth, dude. Smooth move," Andy said, nudging me into Mrs. Fisk's classroom.

"That perfect pass helped me make it happen," I replied before proudly claiming my desk in the middle of the front row.

"There's that boy," Brandon mumbled, taking a seat at the desk to the left of me.

"Brandon Pitts," I grunted, shuffling through my backpack until I found a pen and a pad.

Mrs. Fisk then took complete control of the classroom with one gesture. She raised her left hand, pointing her index finger in the air, and at once, we all knew it was time to pay attention. Mrs. Fisk wasn't like the other teachers. She was an authentic Italian knockout: 5'1", brunette, and sexy from head to toe. When she spoke, everyone listened.

"Today, I want to evoke the creative juices in this classroom. I want you all to write a poem. Write about anything that makes you feel. You have the next thirty minutes to wow me. The timer starts now," she announced before quietly taking a seat at her desk, and my hungry eyes followed her voluptuous frame through every step.

She looked stunning in that flowing baby-blue dress. We immediately began scribbling words into the paper's lines, and while I was writing, I was also thinking, reaching, and dreaming.

"Pass them to the left, and after I've collected all of the poems, I'll review them. In the meantime, open up your study guides and prepare yourselves for the chapter test on Friday."

"*L*, what'd you write about?" Brandon whispered the question, steering my attention away from Mrs. Fisk and those smooth, soft, tree-trunk-shaped calves.

"*L*, are you cool?" he asked again.

I turned to face him, half smiling. "Yeah, *B*, I'm fine. I was just thinking about something. I wrote about a boxer."

"Which one did you write about?"

"John L. Sullivan."

"I've never heard of him."

"He used to fight in the bare-knuckle days."

"Bare-knuckle?"

"During the early days of boxing, athletes used to fight without gloves."

"Wow. I didn't know that."

"I love to study history. My parents call me the history buff, and my family in Chicago calls me the professor."

"Well, they call me B-Kool. That's my rap name."

"You rap?"

"Yeah, I have a studio in my basement."

"You make beats too?"

"Yeah, I love making beats almost as much as I love rapping."

"Class, I need your attention, please," Mrs. Fisk announced, affirming her position in the front of the room. "I am very impressed with a particular student's poem, and with his permission, I'd like him to read it to the class."

The room went quiet.

"Landon Parker, can I request your permission to read your work?"

"Yes, you may," I humbly assured her.

"Did you want me to read it, or are you comfortable reading it yourself?"

"I'd prefer it if you read it," I replied.

"Okay. The title of this poem is 'The Great John L.'"

> There once was a man born with might
> In an Irish house by an Irish light.
> On a cold night when he was four,
> He and his family moved to an American shore.
> There, he became the greatest boxer of all.
> Until gentlemen, Jim, made the poor man fall.

Then he lied all that he could and died just like
they said he would.

The class remained quiet, but I presumed that my poem was a hit, judging by their faces.

"We're running out of time, so you all are now officially dismissed."

The room echoed with ruffling backpacks and shoes squeaking against the floor through the next few minutes.

"Landon, I'd like to talk to you for a moment," Mrs. Fisk's voice stopped me in my tracks.

I walked to her desk, throwing the straps of my backpack over my shoulders.

"That was incredible. You're extremely talented," Mrs. Fisk said with a smile.

"Thank you," I bashfully replied, taking in the scent of her sweet rose perfume.

"It's truly a gift. I'd like to enter your poem in the Sarah Tarpoff Writing Contest."

"That would be great."

"I think you have more than a chance of winning, Landon."

"Thanks."

"No, thank you for sharing your gift with me. Keep writing, young man. Don't ever stop writing."

"I won't."

"Well, you'd better get going before you miss your bus."

"See you later, Mrs. Fisk," I said, waving over my shoulder and walking into the hallway with my head held high.

Brandon met me by the rows of lockers.

"That was dope, *L*. If you can write poetry, then I bet you can also rap."

"I guess so."

"Don't you listen to it?"

"Rap is all I listen to."

"Maybe we should link up."

"Are you saying that you want to start a rap group with me?"

"Yeah, that would be cool."

"What would we call our group?"

"The game is cold right now, and we're two cold cats, so let's call ourselves the Ice Pack."

"That's cold."

"Yeah, too cold," I said as we walked through the sliding glass doors into the chilly December Monday afternoon.

We followed the trails of dew, leading us to the intersection of Fifth and Vine.

"So, *L*, do you freestyle?"

"I love rap as an art form, but I haven't tried it yet. So instead, I write my rhymes."

"That's cool, but freestyling is essential to this art form. You must practice and learn. Soon, it will all come naturally to you. We should cipher."

"Cipher?"

"It's what we call a freestyling session. That's when you spit off the top."

"Okay, I'm all for it. But every rapper needs a name."

"I'm B-Kool, spelled with a *K*."

"That's tight."

"I've been B-Kool for about two years now."

"Well, if you're B-Kool, then I'm Dr. Freeze."

"That's the ticket. I like it."

That's why B-Kool is making power moves.
I'm the type to keep it real smooth; no longer am
    I putting up with their attitudes.
I'm above the rest, taking this to new latitudes.
I'm so high in the sky
I fly above the globe because no matter what,
    B-Kool won't fold
So do what you're told
I've been doing this rap ish since nine years old
I never miss and won't stop shooting for my goals.
Finger grip's kept tight to my nine in my hold,

Never will I feel uneasy in my own home,
Because I know the chrome will put at least two
    to the dome,
I refuse to be just another name left to rot in
    bloodstains,
It's time for Black folks to break the chains,
Trust this game won't be sold for anything,
While I aim, I never will bluff them,
Rapping alongside my light-skinned ruffian,
We keep it tight like cousins; my ninjas aren't
    handcuffing for nothing.
So please don't get to fussing and show respect
    while I'm busting.
Snapping necks while I bust in gunning, and
    when I shoot, they'll be running.
They won't ever see me coming.
These streets know how B-Kool likes to get down.
I'm the king, the king, I'm the king of the under-
    ground sound.

"That was cold, *B*," I said, watching exhaled breath condensate cloud the air.

Yet I was feeling as optimistic as ever. It just felt safe here; it felt like I was beginning the journey to my destiny. I closed my eyes, and then suddenly, I was awakened by the sound of my mother's voice.

"Landon, did you want some breakfast? I made scrambled eggs with cheese and bacon, your favorite." Her voice went singing through the room, ripping me away from the past.

This metamorphosis took me through a swirling journey back into the present. I opened my eyes and sat up, wiping the sweat away from my brow, taking in the sweet scent of applewood bacon. I could hear grease popping while I stood up. Shirtless and unkempt, I casually made my way into the kitchen area, struggling with all of the unanswered questions, doubts, and inconsistencies.

CHAPTER 3

Unraveling the Truth

"Your plates out on the table," Dad announced, resting his powerful forearms on the surface of the kitchen table.

He loved that antique oak wood table, and he would always take the seat by the window. We just knew not to sit there, or at least while he was present. I sat down right beside him, took a deep breath, and then began to devour the food on my plate. I found myself desperately trying not to smack my lips too loud while I was chewing.

"Why are you so fond of this table, Coach?" I asked.

"This table was once owned by your great-grandparents. It's a family heirloom."

"I understand."

"I'm sure you do. Now eat your food without smacking. Don't act like we didn't teach you any manners."

"Don't trip, I'm just a little hungry, that's all, Coach."

"Don't get lost out there in the fast pace of the rat race, never forget to have class. Listen to what I tell you. Always be ready. It's Superman all the time, Landon. There's no place for Clark Kent around here. Oh no, not at all," he said as I eased my back against the chair, hearing the whorls scrape against the flooring.

"So tell me, Dad, what happened?"

"Pat Malkovich once told Mom that we'd never make it out here."

"Wow. He said that to her?"

"Yes, he did. Right in front of Don Behm."

"When?"

"The year was 1986. I believe that incident happened when we first arrived in East Lansing."

"It seems like they were out to get you from the start."

"They were, Landon."

"I wanted to talk about that night."

"You mean the night I spent with Jane Snow?"

"I want to write your story. It's time."

"It is, son. I need to run to the gym right now though. One of my buddies is going to meet me there to train his son. He wants me to show the little guy how to wrestle."

"Okay, when you get back home, then we'll talk about it. I really need to start this novel."

"The story has already begun. Listen and you will learn. Read in between the lines."

"Okay, Dad, whatever you say," I said, lifting the empty plate.

"This is big time. You wouldn't believe what they did to me."

I found myself pressing my fingers against the stainless-steel sink, watching him drive away. I sensed that he had been uncomfortable discussing the details of his case although it seemed a part of him longed to say more. Mom was still asleep in the master bedroom. The TV was blaring as I took a seat in the far right corner of their Jackson Everest sectional sofa, emphasized by rolled arms, bun feet, nail head trim, and matching toss pillows. I let my shoulders fall onto the cushion of the chocolate-colored upholstery and then closed my eyes. In the darkness, I found myself drifting back into the past.

And just when I had fully slipped into a peaceful state, there I was back in East Lansing. I was in the basement of our house at 225 Milford Street. Oh, how I loved being with Phil Parker down in the basement. He was usually too busy coaching, recruiting, and competing to congregate with me. This time, however, I knew that something wasn't right. His eyes were distant, and he was abnormally quiet. He kept gazing at the television screen.

His countenance was melancholy, and his hands were trembling. The tension was rising, and I was becoming restless. I wanted him to tell me that everything was copasetic; I wanted him to wake me from the nightmare unfolding before my very eyes.

"What's wrong, Dad?" I finally blurted out.

I turned to look at him, but he just kept staring blankly ahead for a few awkward moments. Then he turned and reached out for my shoulder.

"Son, something's happened. I need you to keep a secret for me. You can't tell anyone about this. Not even Mom or Ann."

"What? What happened?"

"I made a mistake, and I might have to go away for a little while. I need you to be the man of the house. Please take care of the ladies while I'm away."

"What happened? Why are you going away?"

"One night I went out with this girl, and we had consensual sex. And afterward, she went to the police claiming that I raped her."

"I know that you would never rape anyone."

"No, I would never. I don't understand why she is doing this to me," he muttered.

His lips were trembling, and at that moment, tears were snaking down his cheeks. I had never seen him cry before that; men in my family didn't cry, or at least not in front of us.

"Dad, don't worry. You didn't do it. Remember that you're innocent until proven guilty in a court of law."

"Thanks, Land, you're right. Did you want some chicken? I stopped by the market on the way home because your mom is too weak right now to cook."

"Oh no, I'm good for now, thanks," I replied, sitting up, rubbing my eyes.

I was now back in the present, but through dreams, I found the memories coming back and the truth coming into the light.

"Hey man, are you all right?" Dad said, bolting into the room.

"I'm cool. I must have dozed off. I've been staying up late writing. I believe you, Pop. You're innocent. I want the world to know. I think it's time to clear your name."

"I do too, Landon. I really do."

"Tell me when you're ready. I wanted to ask you a few questions."

"Questions pertaining to the book?"

"Yeah, ever since I started this book. I…"

"What, man?"

"Lately, I've been haunted by these recurring nightmares."

"Well, don't worry anymore. It's time we talk about it. I think it's time to feel pure again."

I sat up, staring ahead, and sure enough, right in front of me on the surface of the coffee table, was my trusty pen and pad. I grabbed the pen, opened the writing pad, and then touched the pen to the paper's lines. Dad was quietly watching the Golden State Warriors play the LA Lakers. It was always a challenge to attract his attention while he was watching sports. He was wearing an ugly Christmas sweater lined with funny pines, misshapen reindeer, and green streaks with some puke-green oversized sweatpants to match.

"Can I ask you a question, Dad?" I asked in a low tone.

He sat there ignoring me, and for a moment, I was a bit unnerved by the awkward silence.

"Dad, what was your greatest accomplishment?" I asked, tapping him on the shoulder.

"What do you think, Landon?" he finally replied, staring blankly ahead.

"I think 'The Hip Concept' was your greatest accomplishment."

"I think you're right, Landon."

"What inspired you to come up with this philosophy of position and control?"

"Well, I had just graduated from Iowa State, and I was coaching alongside Bobby Douglas at UC Santa Barbara. That was when I started to reach deeper. I wanted to understand how to have a definitive advantage over my opponents. Through reading and studying human anatomy, I came up with this road map to success. My goal was to give wrestlers a focal point."

"A focal point?"

"That's correct. Wrestling is a sport of position and control and not the reverse. It's the ultimate sport where there's no external medium between man and his opponent. Examples of this are man and baseball, man and football, or man and basketball. All of these sports have an object that athletes, fans, and coaches alike can target. In wrestling, that medium or focus is the hips. They constitute the focal point, the beginning and the end. Let's focus on four critical areas of 'The Hip Concept,' and discover how each area interrelates to understand the most dynamic and simplified theory available. Phase one is about the hips. The hips are the real focal point. Then we must segment the body into three parts. Position your body on three parts perpendicularly, and you'll learn your most influential position and your opponent's weakest."

"Hip position is always the strongest."

"That's right. Wherever the hips go, the rest of the body must follow because of the attachment. The next phase refers to the theory of above the joints positioning. To gain maximum leverage, you must position any controlling part of the body above the opponent's joints. The third phase explains the concept of inside position, positioning inside the arms or legs. The best way to secure the hips is from the inside."

"You've emphasized the importance of this concept in your summer wrestling camps."

"It was the foundation of the camp curriculum."

"I love 'The Hip Concept.' It has helped me learn how to dominate my opponents by neutralizing their greatest strengths. Without it, I would have been just another wrestler."

"No one knows 'The Hip Concept' like you, Landon."

"All right, Pop, tell me what happened."

"What happened?"

"You know what I'm talking about. It was February 14, 1991. Those were the days when it felt like we were on top of the world. You were the man. You were the head coach of the Spartan Wrestling Team. How'd we fall? How'd it happen?"

"Son, I believe it was a setup."

"A setup?"

"That's exactly what it was."

"Who set you up?"

"It's a complex network of people."

"I will write the story, for our family and our legacy. I want to write this story so that our family can finally heal."

"I will be right back. Want a beer?"

"Yeah, bring me a cold one."

It felt good to let the nape of my neck fall against the cold, smooth leather. I loved visiting my folks. Life was grand when we weren't fussing or arguing. I closed my eyes, imagining the possibilities, and when my eyes reopened, Dad was back in the living room holding two cold beers in hand. He took a seat beside me and then while aiming the universal remote at the television screen, he began surfing through the channels.

"So where were we?"

"We were discussing my new book."

"The book isn't going to be about just the case."

"No?"

"It's about a legacy that began with a poor, Black kid growing up in the late sixties. It's about deceit and betrayal. And it all started when Bobby Douglas introduced me to Dan Severn."

"What does he have to do with this?"

"He wanted to see me fall, and he was willing to do anything to sabotage me."

"I thought Bobby was your friend. I mean, you've known the guy for ages."

"No, Landon, he was jealous. He knew my potential."

"So how does Bobby tie into this?"

"It was Mrs. Douglas that first came to me about this. She approached me at the NCAA tournament and informed me that Bobby knew Severn was untrustworthy long before he referred him to me."

"So through that referral, there were ulterior motives?"

"Whether there were or not, look at how it played out. Who do you think I blame for being that close to a snake in the grass like that?"

"I know who—Bobby *D*."

"I contacted a few law firms last week, and guess who is now interested in taking my case?"

"Who could it be?"

"Drew Cooper and Andings in Grand Rapids, Michigan. They are the same firm that represented those gymnasts in the Larry Nassar case."

"They've already been up against Michigan State."

"They're not just up against Michigan State, no. This time, they're up against Phil Parker."

"So what does Dan Severn 'the Beast' have to do with this?"

"Dan knew my ways. During road trips, I would go out sometimes, and I would ask him if he would join me, but he always deferred."

"He was watching you, Dad."

"He was just an intricate part of the web of deceit."

"So you feel that it was a setup?"

"Yes."

"Then Jane was hired to seduce you?"

"She wasn't a student. What was she doing there, at that particular time in my wrestling room, asking to use the phone?"

"And how did she know the code to get into the door?"

"Her brother rented a property from Grady Peninger. That means she may have been a part of an elaborate conspiracy designed by Peninger to have me expelled from the university."

"And was this brought up in court?"

"No."

"Why didn't Stuart bring this point to the judge?"

"He had ulterior motives."

"What motives?"

"Let's just say he ended up being the Ingham County prosecutor. And through a lot of his cases preceding my trial, he was working directly with Michigan State University."

"It sounds like Michigan State had a lot to lose if you were acquitted."

"They would have been facing a wrongful termination lawsuit. And then a civil rights lawsuit after that."

"And besides, they didn't want the negative publicity either."

"It's a puzzle that's now finally coming together. They wanted to wash their hands of this mess, so they pushed for a conviction and then tried to sweep me under the rug."

"I don't understand how they could ignore the fact that the alleged victim testified not to have been actually raped. I read this not only in her statement to the court but also in her statements to the police."

"They didn't want to hear the truth."

"Justice will prevail, Pop. Don't worry, justice will prevail."

Dad's eyes were hopeful, and at that moment, I felt a secure connection. It was evident in his tone that he believed as I did that we'd overturn this conviction and finally right the wrongs of the past. Now, it wasn't just his fight; it was our fight.

"The presiding judge was Thomas Brown. Brown is a known racist."

"Wow. So how did they set you up?"

"It's quite a story, son. We've got to tell the whole story."

"I need facts. I need names."

"I was doing a clinic in the wrestling room for a troop of boy scouts, teaching them about wrestling, hard work, and dedication. Nancy Larson was there because her sons were a part of the troop."

"Oh, you mean Nancy Larson, Mom's close friend."

"Yeah, she was one of our witnesses in the trial. She later testified in court at the end of the clinic to have seen a woman looking back at her through the overhead windows of the wrestling room door. She looked lost or something."

"Was Jane a student?"

"No, I figured that she must have been working out in the weight room next door. Sometimes, outsiders would come in to use the facilities, but this was rare."

"So how did you two meet initially?"

"I happened to run into her in the hallway while on my way to the office."

"Didn't you find it strange that you just happened to run into her?"

"Come to think of it, yes, but at the time I didn't think anything of it."

"Maybe she was targeting you the whole time."

"She stopped me on the stairs asking if she could use the phone, and naturally, I agreed."

"I took her to the cage where there was the nearest phone, and she made her call. She thanked me and then went on her way. Then the next day, Jane Snow called my office asking me to help her work out. She told me that she wanted me to help her get her butt in shape, so I foolishly agreed to meet up with her. By then, I was falling right into the trap and didn't even know it."

"What happened next?"

Mom suddenly walked into the room wearing a pink robe, tying her wet, long blond hair into a ponytail.

"What are you guys talking about?" she asked with a smile.

Peggy's positivity would light up a whole room, and we fed off her optimism. She kept us focused and gave us strength. Dad looked away for a moment; his eyes were glossy and his thoughts elsewhere. It was evident by his countenance that he was still wrestling with his own emotions, even after all these years.

"The case?" I answered.

"What case?" she asked, scurrying into the kitchen.

"Landon is documenting the rise and fall of Phil Parker."

"That's great. It's about time."

"Yes, Peggy."

"Are you sure that you want to bring those skeletons back out of the closet?"

"Yeah, Mom, we're sure. It's time for the truth to be told. Dad didn't rape anyone, and that's the truth."

"I know, Landon. I testified during the trial. It was a modern-day lynching. Well, I will let you guys get back to business," Mom said.

"Hold on. I've got to use the bathroom," Dad said before standing up and then leaving the room.

I moved into the kitchen where Mom was preparing the water to do the dishes.

"Let me get those dishes for you, Mom," I said with a smile.

"Thanks, Land, but I will do them. You and Dad have some business to attend to."

"No, I insist. You don't need to be standing out here doing the dishes with your back problems and other health complications. I mean, it's a miracle that you're still here. You've been through over twenty-one life-threatening surgeries fighting Crohn's disease and spinal meningitis. It's not fair. Why did so many horrible things have to happen to such a great person?"

"I'm not complaining, Landon. I've lived a great life. I had the best kids in the world. Don't worry about me, Landon."

"I just love you so much, Mom, and I don't want to lose you. I'm not ready to lose you."

"You're not going to lose me."

"I sure hope not."

"So tell me more about this story. Is it for a class project?"

"No, I was thinking about submitting it to the *New Yorker* or something."

"Or maybe you could write a novel."

"Yeah, the story is leading my pen right now. We'll see where it goes."

"The ink will speak volumes. It all happened in 1991. You were just twelve."

"Those were the good ole days."

"Do you want some French toast, Landon?"

"Yes, that sounds great, Mom. You are the best cook in the world."

"Oh, you say that to all your mothers."

We smiled and laughed until Dad's voice summoned me back into the living room.

"Landon, I'm ready," his voice resonated through the house.

"Let's talk," I said, taking a seat beside him on the couch.

He sat back, throwing his arms over his head. "I'm sorry all this had to happen. Sometimes life just isn't fair."

"That doesn't mean that we can't make a change—we must persevere."

"I waited to tell my story because I didn't want to stress your mom. Now she's been told that she has maybe nine months tops to live, and there's no time to wait. We need to do it for her."

"You're right, Dad. It's so hard right now. I love Mom with all my heart. She's the foundation of this family. I'm not ready to lose her."

"I contacted the *State News,* and they agreed to take on the story. They're digging through the case files as we speak."

"That's great. Hopefully, that will lead to your appeal."

"I also contacted a law firm in Grand Rapids, and they scheduled a conference call with me on Wednesday."

"That's exactly the route that we need to be going with this."

"Don't forget my mantra. Carl Adams and I were talking about it yesterday—Superman all the time. We respect and encourage all human beings. We believe in divine power, not steroid power. We will never remove our capes, not morning, noon, or night. We will strive to be more intelligent and tougher than our opponent, and we will neutralize their strength with our hard work and skills. And finally, we will not let our failures stop our hard work so that the next generation will come to know our glory one day."

"I learned to wrestle from your summer wrestling camps. I was out there selling buttons at seven. You know, I used to hate going to camp at first, but the more I went, the more I appreciated being there. It took me a while to realize that I was there to begin the quest to become a champion."

"And that you did."

"I knew it wouldn't be a cakewalk, but it was only pure destiny that led me to that wrestling mat. And win or lose, I learned something new every time."

"Sam was the first of us to earn a state championship. Charles almost did it and then Dennis won the state as a junior."

"You took the state as a senior, right?"

"Yep, and then I took a National Championship securing a full-ride scholarship to Iowa State University."

"I can only imagine the intensity flowing through that cyclone wrestling room during the late sixties."

"It was war all the time. And it was segregated. There was always racial tension in the air, but we all tried our best to come together as a team."

"What was it like being on the same team as the great Dan Gable?"

"Dan rarely spoke to me."

"Didn't you wrestle him in practice?"

"We faced each other only one time."

"What was the outcome?"

"He won thirteen to seven."

"You were part of the greatest wrestling team in history. There are books written about that team."

"Harold Nichols was a good man. Landon, your mother and I have to run a few errands. I need to go by my office real quick to pick up my check, so let's talk more tomorrow."

"That's fine. I will piece together the puzzle and start this novel in the meantime."

"You do that. Start, work on, and complete. Those are the three stages to success."

I watched Dad leave the room while staring blankly at the television screen. I heard him talking to Mom for a while. They're whispering, so I knew that they were discussing either money or Mom's illness. I waited until I heard the garage door close before I decided to head into the study. With pen and pad in hand, I walked into the dimly lit room, sat down at the computer desk, and began right where I left off. After writing for several hours, I made my way into the guest bedroom. The room was cold, and the scent of apple cinnamon lingered through the air. I went for the king-sized bed draped with a thick, fluffy, light-blue comforter and didn't hesitate to plop my tired bones onto the mattress. It felt good to wrap my body in the bedding. I closed my eyes and soon found myself dreaming of a small town called East Lansing—the site where it all began and where it all ended; the place where I had matured from seven to twelve—the place where we lost our innocence.

And there somewhere in those Michigan dreams was a forgotten legacy—a legacy they tried to erase—the legacy of a legend. Their victim was Phil Parker, the legendary coach whom I happen to call my dad. And in my dreams, I'm still there, running down Milford Street thinking about my life, about everything that I longed to be. I rolled to my back and soon was trapped in the darkness, where tall oaks surrounded me; their leaves frosted with snow. And then the night led me deeper into the past. When the smoke finally cleared, I was with Brandon Pitts in the basement of his parents' house. We were at home in the studio, the place where we created pure magic.

CHAPTER 4

———— ✦✦✦✦✦ ————

Redemption

Sweat trickled down my brow as I awakened to the crippling sound of my mother's cries. I always hated it when Mom cried, and I would try to do anything in my power to quell her agony. I found myself looking up at white popcorn ceilings, listening to the pain resonating behind those deep, sobbing moans. It felt as if the roof was caving in on me. I moved to a seated position and then slid to the bedside.

"I love you, Mom," I whispered, holding back the tears, and running my fingertips across my shoulders.

I then stood up and went stammering to the doorway, taking a minute to look at the words bold black ink centered, written on the poster hanging on the wall.

"Do your best and let God do the rest," I whispered aloud while gathering my composure.

I wanted to be strong for her, so she could remember how strong she was. At times, I felt that she was only holding on for us because she had such a sturdy, unafraid resolve, and I always admired her for that. I turned the cold brass knob, opened the door, and made way into the living room following the sound of Mom's cries. I found her by the couch; her sandy, blond hair slightly unkempt, and those rich, jaunty curls dangling. And her knotted hands posted on the arm of the sofa as if they were the only force holding Mom up.

"Momma, are you all right?" I asked, setting my palm gently against the back of her silky, white nightgown.

"No, Landon. I'm in pain. It's Crohn's."

"You've beaten the odds, you're a survivor. You've survived over thirty life-threatening surgeries. You can beat this. Stay strong. I love you. I love you so much."

"I love you too, Land."

"Do you need me to take you to the hospital?"

"No, Land, I'll be all right. It's going away. The pain's going away now."

She slowly stood upright, gathering her composure. She then reached out, taking my hand. I just stood there looking into those piercing blue eyes and found myself peering into tidal waves. She was a master of controlling her own emotions. It was her that taught us to love; it was her that kept us sane. Dressed in a red sweat suit, Dad entered the room abruptly, his brow dripping with sweat.

"Are you all right, Peg?"

"Yes, Phil. I'm fine. I feel faint, that's all."

"Let me help you in the bedroom. You should lie down," Dad replied while carefully leading Mom down the hallway and into the master bedroom.

I took a seat at the couch's edge, staring blankly at the television screen, hoping to convince myself that everything was going to be all right. I kept tapping my toes against the linoleum. It was comforting to know that Mom was still alive. We could see her singing, joking, and offering us words of encouragement. She was Dr. Peggy J. Parker, my own personal psychologist, my confidant, and in my opinion, the best mom in the world. When Dad came back into the room, he was wearing a blank expression. His eyes were glazed, and I could tell that he was starting to lose hope.

"So let's get back to business. I need you to continue telling me your side of the story. Tell me what happened that night."

"Well, Jane called me the next day at my office. I was surprised to hear from her, but I guess, at the time, I didn't think much of it. She said she wanted help weight training, and eventually, the conversation shifted."

"Was it she or you pushing further?"

"I felt like the connection was mutual. We agreed to meet on a Wednesday. So I picked her up at a restaurant that was right by the place that she was living."

"Where did you take her after that?"

"We went to Tangos. When the waiter came, we ordered two Long Island iced teas."

"Did she seem intoxicated after drinking that Long Island iced tea?"

"No."

"Was she stumbling? Or slurring her words?"

"No, she did not seem intoxicated. I didn't think anything of it. She was completely aware and cognizant."

"Go on."

"After we finished our drinks, we left. By the time I pulled onto the main road, Jane was nudging me to pull over so she could use the bathroom. We happened to be right by a house that belonged to one of my close friends, John Snyder. He was a former MSU wrestler. John was making side money by renting the place out to students. I had been there on many occasions, and that was the reason I took her there. I knocked on the door, expecting to see familiar faces, but this time there was a Caucasian guy and a girl that I hadn't seen before to greet me. I asked the young man if John was there, and he said that he wasn't. I then informed them that John happened to be a friend of mine, and I asked them if Jane could come in to use the bathroom real quick. The young man seemed to be losing his patience. He told me that John wasn't there and then slammed the door in our faces. Before I could even plead my case, he had already made up his mind. So on the way back to the car, I noticed that the back door was open, and I led the young girl inside to use the bathroom. After she finished, and we were on our way out, the young man confronted me."

"What did he say?"

"He told me to get out of his house. So we left peacefully."

"Where did you go after that?"

"When we went back to the car, she told me that she wanted to party some more, so I started driving, and we ended up at the Park Inn."

"Did she seem out of it?"

"No, not at all. We parked toward the back of the lot, she let her seat back, and before I even knew it, we were kissing. I unzipped her jeans, and she took them off. After she took her pants off, I climbed on top of her, and we had consensual sex."

"Was she ever asleep during the act?"

"No, she was wide awake the whole time."

"What happened next?"

"She wanted to party, but it was getting late, so I dropped her off at the Silver Dollar Saloon."

"Go on."

"About two weeks later, I was contacted by the police. I received the call from an officer. He asked me if I would come down and talk about an alleged sexual assault. I was shocked. I told them that I wanted to make a statement and then went voluntarily to the station."

"What happened when you got there?"

"They took me into an interrogation room. I still remember how cold it was in that room. Two officers were waiting for me."

"What did they look like?"

"They were middle aged, balding, and White."

"How did they treat you?"

"They played me like a tuba. I felt like the detectives misconstrued my statement."

"You should have spoken to a lawyer before saying anything to them. They were never in your corner."

"The moment that the officer said a local woman accused me of rape, I smelled a setup. Everything just clicked. I mean, I never saw that girl after that. One night ruined my life."

"That's why we're doing this. It's time to tell our story. It's time for the truth to come out."

"Then after the national tournament, during the third week of March, a camera crew from the local news station ambushed me in my office. I was there with my assistant coach, Jesse Reyes. He looked amazed when they shoved the cameras in my face. They were there to talk about a sexual assault allegation. I told them that I would meet them outside in a few minutes, and as soon as they left the room, I hightailed out of the back door. By the time I arrived home, a mob of reporters was waiting with more cameras. I remember your mom telling them to go away. She almost shut her hand in the door while trying to slam it in their faces."

"They were coming after you, and you knew what you were up against."

"Yeah, I knew. I just had to hide out for a while."

This part of the interview was arousing intense emotions in both of us. To evince the truth would be our mission, and I knew, together, we would fight to the day where justice would prevail. The lies had been tormenting us for far too long and, together, we would tread the road of vindication. I found myself glancing down at Dad's hands, and those strong hands that I had admired for so long were now shaking. I thought about the battles his hands had seen, the championships trophies he'd held. I always respected his hands for I knew in my heart that they had toiled the work of legends.

"So tell me what brought you to the Dunnings' law firm?"

"Stuart Dunnings Sr. called me and offered his services."

"When did he call you?"

"About three weeks after the incident."

"How did you feel about Dunnings' law firm initially?"

"I felt confident. They were the best, and I wanted the best. Stuart Sr. once told me that he wanted his son to handle the case. He said that his son was being considered for a high-profile position, and he felt that my case would be his stepping-stone."

"How did you feel about his initial game plan?"

"At first, I was confident in him. I related to the brother because we're both in interracial relationships. I recall him saying something odd while we rode to the preliminary hearing."

"What did he say?"

"He said in a rather deceptive voice that I was going to make him famous."

"Why did you think he would say something like that?"

"I questioned this statement apprehensively because a part of me wanted to trust him."

"How soon did you start to feel that Stuart was providing you with inadequate representation?"

"I began to question Stuart the moment the police called me in and asked me to go to the hospital and take a sample, and he told me to go ahead with them. I couldn't understand why he didn't elect to go there with me. By that time, I was beginning to feel decimated and, for the first time in my life, completely powerless. I was humiliated, and I felt like it was time to end it all. When I would lie down to rest, there was an anvil on my chest. It felt like the weight of the world was on my shoulders, and if it weren't for my family, I don't know if I would have been able to make it through those dark days."

"And to believe, the top prosecutor in the Capital City would be participating in the same criminal acts that he championed a cause against."

"Stuart Dunnings served as the Ingham County prosecutor for nineteen years, and he was the first African American to hold such office."

"I remember those shamed pictures of him coming out of the Clinton County Jail during the midnight hours of September 24, 2017."

"Landon, he looked completely defeated after serving ten months of a twelve-month sentence."

"He was granted early release for good behavior."

"He was wearing slacks and a polo shirt, unbuttoned at the collar, carrying his belongings in a plastic bag. He held on to that bag while making his way to a black sports utility vehicle, and he didn't say a word to the reporters."

"Not a word. Stuart was sentenced at the age of sixty-four to felony misconduct and a misdemeanor charge of engaging in the services of a prostitute."

"They took him down. He was getting away with it for far too long."

"The investigation took one year to bring out the dirt on this guy. Federal, state, and Ingham County officials worked together to bring charges against Dunnings, and they concluded that they could prove he had paid at least five women for sex, over several years. He even used his power of office to force one woman, who was not a prostitute, to let him pay her for sex. The investigators were tipped off during a federal investigation into a sex trafficking ring, and they found Stuart and his brother knee-deep in corruption."

"He was facing up to twenty years in prison on a felony pandering charge when he was arrested in 2016."

"What happened with the pandering charge?"

"He received a lesser sentence as part of a plea agreement with the Michigan Attorney General's Office, who prosecuted his case."

"He was sentenced to three years of probation, and the first was to be served in jail."

"He had been Ingham County's prosecutor since 1997."

"He resigned though, shortly after his arrest."

"And his law license was revoked earlier this year."

"He's still receiving a lovely pension, though."

"The man isn't trustworthy. He wasn't on the right side of the law. And who'd had thought, just five years after my trial date, he would become the new Ingham County prosecutor."

"One of his victims recently came forward to confirm the allegations and tell a story of abuse, drugs, kidnapping, and sexual and mental manipulation. She said that her man went to jail on a drug charge and for abusing her, so she was literally out on the streets and vulnerable prey to a local street thug named Tyron Smith. Smith, known on the streets as T-Bone, is a convicted murderer. Tyron went under police radar after a seventeen-year-old girl that he'd been trafficking was found beaten in East Lansing. She said that T-Bone took her in, got her addicted to crack, and then forced her to prostitute herself in exchange for free drugs and room and board. He told her and the rest of his girls he kept that they owed him, and he made them pay him back by forcing them into a life of prostitution. If they tried to get away, he would beat them and threaten to kill them. And Stuart was one of their main clients."

"Imagine the power that gave him to be putting these girls in front of the head honcho. He and his brother Steven were using and abusing these women."

"He had to have seen the bruises and needle tracks on their skin."

"He saw them. He just didn't care."

"It turns my stomach to think the top prosecutor in the Capital City was engaging in criminal acts, and never once tried to stop it."

"That statement says it all right there, *L*."

"And Stuart had a long record of cracking down on sex trafficking."

"That's the reason why it didn't make sense to many people in the Lansing area."

"He began prosecuting prostitution cases after his election to the prosecutor's office in 1996. And starting in 1997, he used the power of the courts to impound the vehicles of those accused of purchasing sex and sought felony charges for women who had two or more previous prostitution convictions."

"What a hypocrite."

"There's more. Stuart ran three successful prosecutions against three sex traffickers. Two men and one woman were convicted of transporting underage women across the state line for the sole purpose of selling their bodies into the ugly world of prostitution."

"How's anyone to know?"

"It's a web of deceit that we're just beginning to unravel."

"That it is indeed. Well, Landon, Mom and I are going to ride to my office to pick up my check."

"Okay, no problem."

"We'll continue our conversation later."

"It's mind-boggling to think this went on for so long, and no one did anything."

"They needed cold, hard evidence."

"And that's exactly what they lacked in your case—cold, hard evidence. Where's the evidence to support Jane's statement that she passed out during, before, or after having sex with you?"

"The evidence does not exist. It's not in the transcripts or the statements provided by the alleged victim. This case was built, tried, and won on the grounds of one person's word against the other. And the more I look at the alleged victim's behavior before and after the alleged incident, the more I see a setup unfolding."

"I mean, why would anyone go barhopping and then continue drinking after allegedly being so drunk that they couldn't even lift their hands just minutes before?"

"It was a witch hunt. It was a case of old-fashioned militia justice."

"They set you up, Dad."

"They sure did."

"It's time to tell our side of the story."

"Our side of the story has never been told until now," Dad said, reaching into his leather attaché.

"What was life like behind bars?"

"I wrote it all down," he said, running his fingertips against his beard's stubble.

"What?"

"During my incarceration, I kept a diary."

"I look forward to reading it."

"You will. I will see you later, Landon."

"Are you sure that Mom's all right to go with you?"

"Yeah, she's fine. I know my wife. She just enjoys the ride."

"All right, you keep on believing, Dad," I said, watching him walk out of the room.

And when the front doors closed and the sound of feet scurrying ceased, I soon found myself staring into the television screen, but I wasn't watching anymore. I was thinking about the controversy surrounding the case. I thought about how humiliating it would be for my dad to have to live this incessant nightmare over and over again. He carried the invariable weight on his shoulders for years, when in his heart of hearts knew that he was innocent of the charges. The truth is that Jane wasn't asleep or unconscious. Jane didn't say no—she came on to him and was a willing participant in the sex act. Thus, the justice system tainted its purity in the case and has debased the character of a legend. Phil was held in contempt and made to suffer disparagement and mockery.

These allegations have destroyed a legacy dating back to the late 1960s. I intend to contest these untruths with the pen and with the actual truth. With this story, I aimed to bring honor back to our family name, and the more I wrote, the more I believed in my father's innocence. After writing for several hours, I eased back against the couch cushions and fell fast asleep.

CHAPTER 5

The Trail to the Trial

Arizona State University officially accepted Mom's internship proposal, and I felt eager to put the scandal behind us. Our new life was to begin in Tucson, Arizona. Tucson brought us closer to my mother's side of the family, and a part of me had always dreamt of living out in sunny California. For a while, I held on to the years we spent there in Lansing, flourishing, learning, and building our dreams. Everything we had once known was now becoming a distant memory. Mom, Dad, and Ann seemed so confident and optimistic. I fed off their positive vibes, and soon I, too, was sure that everything would go back to some sense of normalcy. I was convinced that justice would prevail.

I remember my last week at Hannah Middle School. By that time, friends were barely even friends anymore. Everyone knew I was leaving, and maybe they didn't want to get too attached; besides, they already had their prepuberty adolescent worries to overcome. I spent my last day of school quietly saying goodbye to friends and to everyone whom I had spent the past five years learning with. A part of me knew it was the open fields, rolling hills, and the small-town atmosphere of East Lansing that I would miss the most. It was as if somehow, I knew that ten years would pass before I would make the trip back to Lansing. And soon enough, we were packed and leaving it all behind. In the front seats, my parents quietly conversed about the trial. They discussed the allegations, and they talked about the people who turned their backs on us. We wanted to put that ordeal in the past, and we were confident that Dad would be exonerated.

We rented a condo on the outskirts of Tucson's eastside. Being away from it all was paradise. I felt safe for a while in that lonely, desert neighborhood. I took on a new identity when I entered Macdonald Middle School as the awkward, skinny new kid on the block. By that time, I was already an award-winning poet, and for a poet, the desert provided a symphony of analogies just waiting to hatch into the paper's lines. I loved the change in scenery. Those dry mountains peeking through the distance, the spiky cacti scattered along the terrain, and the ravines and dry washes told their own stories. Arizona evoked many wild dreams during those cold Tucson nights. I was getting taller, and a peach-fuzz mustache sprouted over my lip. With every passing day, we became mentally and spiritually stronger. The trials and tribulations only brought us closer as a family. We decided to put aside our petty differences and let those old grudges go.

I knew wisdom could protect me emotionally from falling victim to what happened to my dad in Michigan. I wrote poems over many long, arduous months, and by midyear, I won the National Council of Teachers Award for excellence in writing. I learned how to turn depression into passion—one that would only fuel my pen to continue the fight. I rarely saw the California side of the family and was excited about getting to know them better. When I arrived for my first day of school, I found that I was the only African American student in the eighth grade. I was left to bear the brunt of ignorance and hate. They always seemed to bring me down, although I wouldn't let their lies destroy me. I wanted to seclude myself from the hate, whether it was from classmates, so-called friends, or even family members. There seemed to be harsh words, cold gestures, and many verbal attacks everywhere I turned.

Being the son of a coach, I knew the importance of confidence, and without faith, I felt like a shell of a young man. So I learned how to shut out the cruel words of others because with confidence, I had the advantage over them. With self-belief on my side, I knew that there was no stopping my progression. With high self-esteem, it was only a matter of time for all of my greatest dreams to come to fruition. I was always a loner and a rebel, so fitting in, to me, was an unimportant ritual. Still, I kept at least a few real friends by my side because no one is an island.

That summer was as hot as ever. Ann and I shared one room, and my parents were to share the master bedroom. I was content to be there in Arizona. There was a clean scent in the air, and we all longed to get clean. We wanted to get as far away as we could from those allegations looming in Michigan, where my dad was fighting for his freedom. We were counting the days to Dad's trial. At fourteen, I still believed in the justice system. Since the very beginning, I felt that my dad was innocent of the charges. The truth festered in the details behind his charges. Clearly the prosecution lacked sufficient evidence to have proven their case beyond a reasonable doubt.

There was no evidence of any date rape drug in the toxicology reports, and that's just the undeniable truth. Jane Snow herself even stated in court, under oath, that she never felt as if she was raped. Maybe she had gone too far to turn back, or perhaps she was just a pawn in a game of slander and false allegations. Either way, I knew how hard my dad had worked to earn the position as the head coach of the Michigan State Wrestling Team. It took a lifetime of dedication to get there, and still, he strove to achieve more. Dad's journey transcended Phil the athlete. He was Coach Parker, a coach well on his way to becoming a hall of famer, and in one night, it was all taken away. To believe, in one night, an entire career shattered into a million pieces. I now relied on the justice system to see through manipulations and lies.

We often frequented the Mi Nidito restaurant during our trips to Nogales, Mexico, at weekends. We found ways to drown out the negativity going on in our lives. And soon enough, it was time for Mom and Dad to fly back to Lansing for the trial. My grandparents made the trip down from California to watch over us while our parents were away. I remained optimistic throughout the trial. Never did I ponder the notion that we as a family would lose anything else besides the life we left behind. I was busy finding out who I would become on the journey from boyhood to manhood. I felt obligated to be like my dad, the hero whom I had admired, whom I always longed to become. Ann and I went back to La Mirada with my grandparents and even to Lake Almanor with the Phelans. That was the last time I made the trip to Lake Almanor with the family.

I still remember the day that the verdict was announced in my dad's case. I was out in the backyard of our townhouse in Tucson, Arizona, flipping a coin. If the coin landed on heads, he would be found not guilty, tails and he would be found guilty. I flicked the quarter into the air until it hit the ground—tails. Suddenly, the sliding glass door opened, and by the look on Ann's face, I already knew.

"Dad was found guilty," she said, her voice shuddering under trembling lips.

I held back the tears because I wanted to be strong for them. Dad prepared me for this back in East Lansing, and during our talk in the basement, I made a promise that I would take care of the two ladies in our life in his absence.

We made a pact back when this nightmare began. I intended to keep that promise by being the man of the house while he was gone. I remember finding Mom crying in her room that night. I tried to console her, but I didn't have to worry about Momma. She had a fantastic resolve and an immeasurable inner strength. Being the best psychologist in the world probably helped her cope with the heavy burdens that she carried in her life. I watched her suffering through her battle with Crohn's disease and the constant pain that came along with it, and she never once let it break her spirit. Even after being maimed by surgeries and barely able to stand up straight, she was still as proud and beautiful as ever. She didn't care about the negative things people had to say about her. She understood the human psyche, and she would always find a way to forgive.

When I entered our condominium, I could hear Mom sobbing. That was the only time I had seen her cry throughout the trial. I asked her if she thought Dad could make it through his time in jail, and she assured me that she knew he would persevere. She was more concerned about how Dad would take losing his career and everything he had worked for—everything he had earned and everything he was. She was worried that he would lose his pride; and I assured her that Dad was a legend, and what he had earned could not be erased.

Mom's drabness quickly turned into joviality because, at that moment, we both agreed that Phil Parker was going to make it. He would be intrepid and fearless through the entire ordeal, and in the whole gamut of things, this would only make us stronger. We all had plenty of life yet to live, and we wouldn't let this stop us. We garnered the strength, love, and compassion needed to pull through this troubling time. We then joined hands and collectively made a pact not to let anything break us apart. I knew that those iniquitous charges would be challenged, and one day we would unite as a family again. Suddenly, the memories faded into darkness, and I was floating through a lucid dream environment. I felt like I was in a parallel universe, gripping a silver umbilical cord. My hands burned while kneading my palms across its thick fibers, narrowing the distance between my dream state and the physical world.

"Wake up, Landon!" Dad's voice chimed in, pulling me through the doorway of spiritual travel.

I then opened my eyes, lying on the corner wedge of the sectional couch, sliding my fingertips across the chocolate-colored nailhead trim.

"Sorry, I must have dozed off," I replied, rubbing my eyes.

"It's an hour past noon, and you're still sleeping?" he grunted, standing over me, holding a stack of legal pads under his right arm. He was shirtless, and his light-blue gym shorts were soaking with sweat.

"I've been staying up late night after night."

"Doing what?"

"Writing, Dad. This book isn't going to write itself," I said, moving to the edge of the couch.

"That's great. Keep up the good work."

"I will."

"Here's my complete diary from jail. Hopefully, it will provide you with some insight," Dad said, setting the pads on the surface of the coffee table.

"Thank you. This is just what I needed to dive deeper into the case."

"This is it, Landon. This is your opportunity to shine. This is our story, and if we don't tell it, then it won't ever be told."

"This story has a special hold on me."

"How's that, Landon?"

"I've been experiencing these vivid dreams, sometimes even while I'm partially awake," I admitted, staring blankly ahead.

"You're having nightmares?"

"No, they're just dreams. And these dreams come in the form of memories. It seems that every time I close my eyes, there I am, again, in a dream world."

"That's how we dream sometimes."

"No, this is different."

"Maybe the universe is guiding you through this journey. That's how things happen when you're following your destiny."

"I was born to write this story."

"That, you were, Landon," he said, moving into the kitchen, leaving me alone in the living room.

I couldn't wait to dive into the pages of his diaries. I looked down at my parents' Amish Lancaster mission table, my reflection staring back at me in the tempered glass, thinking, reminiscing, and drifting. I could smell the scent of maple wood in the air as I opened up the first of four legal pads and found myself, once again, slipping into an oneiric state. My body was accustoming itself to the realm of astral travel, so it was easy for me to move into wakeful consciousness. I wanted to know what life was like for Phil Parker during his incarceration; I wanted to know where it all went wrong. The dreams were pulling me out of the physical world, and while my eyes followed the lines, I was again in another realm, watching our story unfold in real time.

Photo credit: The State News (Newspaper)

+ + + + + +

CHAPTER 6

Life after the Verdict

Phil

October 20, 1992

I am now officially an inmate in the Mason County Jail. I have been placed in position 3C-4 and housed with a nineteen-year-old White male named Tony. I was looking back at the scared five-foot-three kid with sandy, blond hair and a faint peach-fuzz mustache. He is shaking like a leaf, and I was feeling sorry for him. His confinement is due to burglary charges. One of the hardest things to contend with is the repulsive and redundant food selection. Today, I went to the law library to search for holes in the prosecution's case. How could this have happened to me? This question keeps running through my mind, and I am determined to prove my innocence. I returned, exercised, and then found myself glued to the TV, watching *Sally Jessy Raphael*. David Garner showed up to visit me later that day. We talked for a while. I tried my best to remain as optimistic as possible, although I was crumbling inside. And everywhere I looked, those cold walls surrounded me. David is 5'2", thin, middle aged, and wealthy. His dark hair is tied in a ponytail, and he's wearing a white T-shirt and oversized denim blue jeans. His face is clean-shaven, and his squinty, brown eyes are bloodshot red.

"So how are you holding up, Phil?" David asked as I looked back at him through the plate glass, feeling relieved to see a familiar face.

"It's a real struggle, man. I can't believe I'm here when I know that I'm innocent."

"Phil, you know that in your heart. I know you're innocent. The next step is to appeal. You need to put all your energy into that right now."

"You're right, Dave. Thanks for coming to visit me."

"You keep your head up, Phil."

"I will, Dave."

I stretched out with Bremmy Hook. He is one of the few White inmates who wished to bridge the racial divide. I'm at least ten years his senior, but he looks older than me. Maybe it's the salt-and-pepper gray hair or the crow's feet around his eyelids that make him look so weathered by the years. I read the *Lansing State Journal*, trying to get my mind off my case. After I had skimmed through the sports page, I played basketball. During the two-on-two game, I crossed paths with one inmate who seemed to enjoy walking the fine line. Gene is tall, athletic, and mean. He likes to play the leader and would proclaim to be the most formidable White man alive. Gene tries to be intimidating by scolding me. I longed to snatch him by his wild crimson hair and smash his face, but to survive this hellhole, I had to keep my eyes on the prize.

And it's the little things that I must hold on to during those turbulent times when walking on a tightrope. A part of me was always ready to snap, but I couldn't let myself go there. We had our whites washed today, and that was enough resolution to keep me on the straight and narrow path for a while. I read a few passages from the Bible before writing to Landon, Ann, and Peggy until the lights went out.

October 28, 1992

I spoke to Mom and Terry briefly, stretched out, and wrote letters to George Patterson, Susan Contreras, and David. I asked Sellik to turn on the television at approximately 7:10 a.m., but he didn't turn it on until eight forty-five. Deputy Sellik had a short fuse today. He got a kite from Lt. Visero, issuing complaints about my media visits. I was thrilled to have received letters from both Landon and Ann. They are my hope and why I must fight on. They are the reason why I will never give up until my name's cleared.

The hours seemed to drag on as I moved deeper into my stay. I tried my best to enjoy the bologna and mushroom soup provided by the correctional facility, despite the consternation always brewing around me. I couldn't stop thinking about my meeting with Stuart last week. He assured me that he'd be there on the appeal if I still wanted him. Although he seemed sincere, I found myself questioning if he had my best interests in mind. Why did he make me take the stand unprepared? I'm beginning to wonder just whose side he was on.

"Parker," Lt. Visero said, approaching me from behind.

His thin face though roughly aged by the years, struck pure fear in its wake. Freckled skin on his chin loosely sagged around his neck, and he had this bushy brown mustache that covered his top lip completely. Visero walked with a limp, and when he was angry, his beady brown eyes twitched sporadically.

"Yes?" I replied, turning to face him.

"Your lawyer is on the phone. Come with me," he grunted as I left my tray at the table and followed Visero's lead. "Here, make it quick," he said, handing me the phone.

"Phil, how are you holding up in there?" Stuart asked in a low tone.

"As good as I can."

"Tell me about Loretta Williams. I'm sorry you mentioned her during the meeting, but my thoughts were elsewhere."

"She's one of the jurors that they dismissed. I happened to run into her in a chance encounter shortly after the trial. She noted that I looked pale and then she took my hand, looked me in the eyes, and told me that I never had a chance."

"And she was one of the Black jurors, I suspect?"

"Yes, she was. Also, I spoke to Jeff Parrot of the *State News* about his absence yesterday, and he informed me that he was denied access by receiving. I wrote a kite to Major Carpenter specifying the criteria for media access."

"Are you sure that you're ready to talk to the press right now, Phil?"

"You don't think it's a good idea?"

"It's all about strategy right now, Phil."

"Strategy?"

"Right on."

"I talked to Nick yesterday. He was very inspiring and supportive."

"Nick?"

"Harold Nichols, the legendary coach of the Iowa State Cyclones."

"Oh, you're referring to your former college wrestling coach."

"Nick is all right with me."

"Well, Phil, I've got to run. Keep your head up. I will be in touch."

I gave the officer the phone and then followed Visero back to C-block.

October 29, 1992

Today I stretched out, wrestled with Jasper, ate spaghetti for dinner, and then read the "Book of Numbers" in the Bible. Sellik cut the television off at 10:00 p.m., but I went to sleep happily, knowing that I had received a new pair of pants today. Dale Sellik is about 5'11", with a medium build. He's in his early forties, and his hair has already turned a dusty-silver shade. He has a long, thin nose and a short chin. They can take away my freedom, but they will never take my dignity. I found myself tossing and turning on my bunk. The various faces staring back at me in this life behind the walls are devoid of emotions. It's so hard to feel in prison. When it gets too challenging to cope, I think of my family awaiting my return; they comfort me. I try not to think about how much I had lost in an instant.

It's all coming into focus now. I am determined to piece together those shattered pieces of my life. I must expose the truth because only the truth will set me free.

October 30, 1992

I awoke staring up at the cold prison ceiling, wishing I were somewhere else. After stretching out, I did push-ups until my arms went numb. Meanwhile, Jasper and Brian got into an argument over the heating system. Brian is young, White, and crazy as hell. Jasper seemed to tower over the five-foot-two, blue-eyed maniac. Jasper's tall and light-skinned. He has high cheekbones and a pug nose. Jasper wanted warmth, but Brian just wasn't willing to budge. Later that day, my friend Judy Becker came to visit.

"So, Phil, how are you doing?" she asked with a hint of a smile spreading across her short, round face.

She looked divine sitting on the other side of the glass partition. Judy was petite, but she would light up a room with her presence. She wore her silky brown hair sectioned into diamond shapes and then twisted into tight little knots.

"I'm doing my best," I replied.

"I know. It's not fair. It's just not fair. Well, hang in there, Phil," Judy moved near the glass, and I knew at once she wanted to tell me something.

Tiny embers were burning in those almond-shaped hazel eyes. She hesitated for a moment and then shuddered. She looked confused while silently batting those long curly eyelashes. It was comforting to see her sitting there in that elegant emerald-green dress. And maybe it was the green in her dress that reminded me of what they took from me. I made a promise to myself to one day let the world know the truth. I would surely take back my pride and my legacy.

Judy removed her blue wire-rimmed glasses and then looked at me with quivering eyes.

"I spoke to her, Phil."

"Who?"

"Jane."

"When?"

"We spoke before the trial. I called Jane one night, and I asked her to tell me why."

"And how did she respond?"

"She said that she wasn't intending on going through with it. She just wanted to make you sweat a little."

"Wow."

"It's wrong, Phil. It's so damn wrong."

"Don't worry. I'm going to pull through this."

"I'm here for you, Phil. We support you. I just wanted you to know that."

"Thanks, Judy."

"You're innocent. We both know who was wrong in this case," she said, looking away.

October 31, 1992

I stretched out and read letters from Etta, but the whole time I was thinking about my conversation with Frawley last week. I needed to come up with five grand or expect a court-appointed lawyer to handle my appeal. A good talk with the newbie, George, distracted me from my problems for a while. George Songs is one of the youngest and meanest inmates on the block. He's short, stocky, light-skinned, and rangy. George is twenty-one and likes to wear his greasy, straight brown hair twisted in tight cornrow braids most of the time. His light-brown eyes sparkle when he speaks about how much he loves his girlfriend. He talked about his thirst to kiss her and of his dreams about making love to his "Baby Doll." He has another girl in Battle Creek on the side, but she didn't fill the void in his life quite like his lady. Clinton just won the presidency, and America is making a dramatic shift toward more democratic ideals. I spoke with Peggy this morning. She sounded optimistic, as always. Oh, how I needed to hear her voice. Time is moving so fast, and life behind the walls is becoming just a blur of repetitions. Before I know it, my stay will have dwindled to the last day. Soon, I will be free again. I refused ever to let this calamity break my spirit.

November 1, 1992

After I worked out, I called Peggy, and we spoke briefly about her former boss, David Garner. Then at approximately two thirty in the morning, a man named Jerry Gallagher approached my suite and wanted to talk. Jerry is taller than most of the guards. This former marine walks like a general and always has his brown hair buzzed low. Somewhere in his mind, he is still active in the military, and according to him, we are all under his control. Gallagher speaks with a Southern drawl even though he had never been anywhere near the South. Gallagher's boyish good looks made him stand apart from the rest.

"Parker, I'm Jerry Gallagher. I know Nancy Larson. She's a real class act. But listen, I made a promise to her that I would get in touch with you, and I'm a man of my word."

"Yes, I know Nancy. What is this about?"

"Follow me. I know a place where we can talk."

I followed his lead through empty, white hallways. For some reason, I felt as if he was someone that I could trust. He soon directed me into the conference room.

"Phil, there are officers around here that you don't even know who couldn't believe the verdict."

"I still can't believe it myself."

"It's a complete farce, a setup. We'll talk more when it's safe. I just wanted you to know that I know you didn't do it."

"What happened in my car that night was undoubtedly consensual. It was consensual sex between two consenting adults. She even testified that she never said no. She never passed out nor was she stumbling or slurring her words. The next day, the girl just turned on me. Someone wanted me out, and maybe they used her as a pawn. Hell, I think they used us both."

"I know, Phil. We will talk more soon."

"Thanks, man."

"Thanks for what?"

"Thanks for this. I needed this. I needed to hear the truth for once. Now, I know that I will make it through this nightmare."

November 2, 1992

Today, I'm beginning to realize what it means to be a prisoner, but I don't feel institutionalized like some of the other inmates around me. It's day one for me on Post One, Dorm C. There's a murderer on this block. He's White, tall, stocky, over the hill, and irritable. They say he shot a Black infant to death, yet they sentenced him to work release? He hardly comes out of his cell. Today, I worked out, read the paper, and spoke to my sister Terry, Adley, and my wife, Peggy. It's comforting to hear their voices and words of encouragement. Peggy is distraught because her former boss, David, is pressing her to the point of harassment. He's looking for someone to save him from his legal issues, and she's not willing to jeopardize her reputation or the reputation of her close friends. I think she wants me to intervene. I want to be there for her, but I'm powerless behind these cold jailhouse walls.

November 3, 1992

This morning was colder than the rest. You could almost feel the frost in the air. There's a strange mix of inmates here. Seven Blacks, two Mexicans, and twenty-two Whites house the block. You can feel the tension around some of the Whites. I signed up for church, but we didn't have it today. So after the sermon, I stretched out and then ate ham and yams for lunch. Behind these walls, this type of meal is a delicacy. Jervis is going on about an affair, and soon enough, his raspy voice has taken over the mess hall. Jewish by birth, Jervis was chubby and rubicund. He had stringy, reddish-brown hair and broad shoulders.

"Now listen up y'all. This chick just showed up at my house. I was having an affair with her, and she just showed up out of the blue. I guess she met my wife while I was sleeping. And check this y'all, I not only banged her, but I also banged her friend, and this chick was the best I ever had. Her skin's smooth as porcelain, and believe me, she's tall and sexy—the Amazon woman type. She was in a wheelchair at the time but man, was she a firecracker."

After he told his story, we laughed, grunted, and then went back to plunging our forks back into those sweet, precious yams. The taste of sweet potato was making me long to be back at home.

November 4, 1992

Today I worked out near Oscar, a forty-five-year-old Mexican inmate. Oscar is working out harder than usual in the lounge. I watched him out of the corner of my eye, staring menacingly at me. Given that he's 6'1" and over 285 pounds, he likes to push his weight around. His shaved head shone in the dim light above while he stood there curling the iron. I remember thinking that there might be an eventual showdown between us.

After my workout, I read an article about Magic Johnson in the *State Journal*, and suddenly, the shortest White inmate in the dorm, freckle-faced Ray, jumps up in front of the television. Ray has dark-brown hair, a heavy build, and sharp features. He wanted to watch cartoons, so all of us were being forced to yield to his preference. I guess it doesn't matter what is polite or decent because only the strong will survive here. A few hours later, I spoke to David and informed him that Peggy had sent a letter to explain her stand on his requests and legal issues. After talking to David, Jasper and I got into a conversation about old flames. I remember us laughing like fools until the lights went out.

CHAPTER 7

Hard Time

November 11, 1992

I took Ray to work out with me. This strategy is to deter him from controlling the television. At 8:00 a.m., he always insists on watching cartoons, whereas I want to watch "*Good Morning America.*" This morning, Jasper helped me distract him. After TV time, I called home and spoke with Landon. He said that a rat had invaded their condominium. A few hours later, I made a call to Sam.

"Hey, bro."

"How are you holding up in there, Phil?"

"I'm all right. Say, bro, I need you to do me a favor."

"What is it, Phil?"

"I need you to send Peggy some money."

"No problem, bro."

"Thanks, man."

"We're family."

"Right on."

"Hey."

"What?"

"Don't feel so alone in there, man. We're with you. We're all with you."

"Thanks, Sammy."

After my conversation with Sam, we were watching TV, and racial tensions escalated. It was seven o'clock in the evening, and we were in the day room watching the *Bills v. Pittsburgh* when all of a sudden, Hank strutted into the room huffing and puffing. Hank Slice is doing a lifetime bid for attempted murder. He's 5'9" and built like a tank. Slice likes to show off by screaming in the weight room. Hank's shaved head and wild brown beard make him look a little rough around the edges. The mood in the room shifted as he waltzed up to the television.

"I don't have any time to watch this crap. Hogan's Heroes is on!" he grunted, reaching out for the dial.

"Don't touch that. You're in the wrong cell, Hank. Look around. We want to watch the football game, and that's what we're going to do!" I said, standing up and squaring my feet.

Hank stared me down for a while before reluctantly deciding to concede.

November 12, 1992

Brian Babcock was released today. I guess leaving this place was tough for him because they screwed up his release. Brian and I used to talk in the mess hall from time to time. He is one of the shortest inmates and also one of the funniest. I'd bet all the money on my books that Babcock would make anyone laugh. In here, he's our own blue-eyed, blond version of Eddie Murphy. Brian, despite being twenty-four, already shows wisps of gray in his bushy crop top. His primary source of pride is an ugly scar that stretches down his left cheek. It's his unofficial badge of honor. He gave me his blanket on one occasion, and behind these cold walls, that means something. I was grateful that night to have used them to better cushion my bed. Peggy's close friend, Etta Rosenthal, came to visit me a few hours later. Etta was fine featured, and her complexion held a healthy olive tone. She had short black hair and was wearing a long, black sleeveless dress. Her dark-blue two-inch heels clicked against the floor until Mrs. Rosenthal had slipped into the chair behind the glass. We talked for a while, and before she exited the visitation area, Etta promised she would send a copy of *Newsweek Magazine*. As she left, Alvin showed up unexpectedly. Alvin Riley was the best man at my wedding, and now he's attending medical school at Michigan State University. He seemed to be at least ten pounds lighter than the last time we'd met. Alvin is tall, dark-skinned, and hefty. He was wearing a black sweater and blue jeans.

"Hey, man."

"It's tough to see you in here like this, Phil," he said in a low tone.

"Don't worry about me. I'll be fine. So, Alvin, I heard that you moved?"

"Yeah, I'll give you my new address."

"How's everything with you, my brother?"

"Good. I'm working at Lansing General right now."

"That's good. Well, take care of yourself, Al."

"You too, Phil."

After I met with Alvin, I watched the Pistons play the Bulls. Jordan won the game in the last

four seconds, but Ms. Carlotta, one of the few
African American guards, locked us in the room
and made us miss a vast majority of the fourth
quarter. She was short and rotund but very
attractive. These were among the many freedoms
I longed to get back. It was the little things that
reminded us that we weren't free anymore. I spent
hours tossing and turning on my bunk while a
group of young African American inmates played
cards until the lights went out.

November 13, 1992

I called Rev. Graves to find out about Juror
Irma Washington. He wasn't available. I finally
received Peggy's letter at ten in the morning.
Landon and Ann were fighting over a sweatshirt.
They shouldn't allow trivial things to break their
family ties. Blood is thicker than water, and that
is what I always taught them.

Riddick Bowe fights Evander Holyfield
tonight, and I'm excited to hear the outcome.
It snowed hard today in Lansing, at least four
inches deep, and it's painfully cold. This morning, the tension eased when Jasper accidentally
opened up the door on an inmate using the bathroom. We all cracked up and then ate Cheerios
for breakfast, fish sandwiches for lunch, and
hamburgers for dinner. Dave, the new guy on the
block, is already testing my patience. He walks
past my door every morning. Dave is of Scotch
Irish descent. He is tall, dark-haired, and muscular. His left leg is significantly shorter than the
right causing him to drag his feet with every step.
I guess that's his way of exercising. Cesar, the forty-five-year-old Mexican, keeps doing push-ups

while I'm reading the paper, and it's driving me crazy. Cesar always wears a fishnet stocking cap over his slicked-back black hair. He's prideful, but I see right through him. Behind that façade, he's just another scared, confused lost soul. *Malcolm X*, the movie, starts Wednesday, and the city of Flint banned its showing. I can feel the tension in the air with the Whites. Some didn't want to watch *ESPN*, but we refused to turn the channel, and though we are on the brink of war, everyone kept the peace today.

November 16, 1992

After stretching, I did my daily routine of push-ups and sit-ups. Unfortunately, they didn't let us go to the gym today because of power failure throughout the city. I got a haircut in the morning and then spoke with Terry and my dad in the afternoon. Dad's sick, but he's a fighter. I'm confident that he'll beat this. They roused us up at 11:30 a.m. due to a supposed fire drill, but I know they placed us in the gymnasium to go through our rooms and ascertain drugs. Dogs sniffed out our cells, and within minutes, the guards carted off several Caucasian inmates while we were in the gymnasium.

An hour later, Stuart came to visit, and we both signed the appeal paperwork. Before our meeting, I spoke with Dad. He is in good spirits. After our conversation, I watched Miami and Buffalo play, feeling numb. I don't know who won because the lights went out at 11:00 p.m., so I just laid there for a while, wishing I could fly away.

November 17, 1992

It's seven thirty in the morning, and I just learned that Lt. Hill, a young Black female deputy, did not allow entry to two of my visitors because they were not on the list. I feel this is a grave mistake on the jail's behalf as they didn't even attempt to contact me. I filed a kite for the third time for their incompetence. My spirits are up a little because today, I finally had my appeal forms notarized. I stretched much longer than usual since we didn't attend the gym. Later, I spoke with Peggy and then I talked to my old friend Tom.

"Hey, *T.*"

"Phil, I'm headed to New Jersey right now."

"Jersey, huh?"

"Yeah, yeah, yeah, I'm going to visit my boy, G-Money. That boy *G*'s so skinny he can barely hold up his clothes."

"Skinny, huh?"

"Yeah, he's a stand-up kind of guy."

"Yeah?"

"You don't belong there, Phil."

"You know what happened, but I'll tell you one thing."

"What's that, *P*?"

"One day, the wrongs will be righted. One day, the truth will prevail. I assure you of that."

"I know, man. You keep on believing."

"I won't ever stop."

"I know you won't, Phil."

"Take care."

I clung to the moment, standing by the phone, smiling. I was relieved to talk to a friend, someone who knew me. It was approximately eight thirty when Deputy Red woke me up and escorted me into his office. Red was blue in the face, and while he spoke, the loose skin under his jaw flapped. Red had just turned fifty-two, and he looked even too frail to hold up his uniform.

"Did you contact *Channel 6*?" he asked in a low tone.

I hesitated for a moment, questioning the reasoning behind the question. "Why?"

"Don't play dumb with me. Why did we receive a call from *Channel 6*?" He moved to the wall and shut the sliding glass window. "Look, Phil. I'm not here to play games. When an officer asks you a question, I expect an answer from you."

I sat there, stunned at his approach to me. "I'm not sure what your reasoning is."

"Well, what did I ask?"

"You wanted to know if I contacted *Channel 6*."

"They called me, and I'm trying to arrange things. But I told you, I'm in no mood for games."

"I'm not playing games."

"You have the right to interview."

"Well, then?"

"You're playing games right now. Go back to your cell," Red grunted, folding his arms over his chest.

I then walked away, and approximately ten minutes later was alerted over the loudspeaker that my interview would be at around 10:00 a.m. tomorrow. So I spent the rest of the evening writing and sending out letters to the civil rights attorney, Rev. Grace, and my lovely wife, the love of my life, Peggy.

November 24, 1992

Maria, from *Channel 6 News,* came in today to interview me to assess the trial. Deputy Red escorted me to the library. Maria Gonzalez was waiting at the table, her paperwork strewn out in front of her. She was wearing a green turtleneck sweater and blue jeans. I admired her long, flowing black hair complemented by those high cheekbones and attractive features. I sat across from her, clasping my hands.

"I'm Phil Parker. Nice to meet you."

"I know. I'm Maria, from *Channel 6 News.*"

"Everyone knows by now. Thank you for coming out to talk to me today."

"You're welcome—we're here for the facts."

"The facts will lead straight to justice because this is a case of complete injustice. A misled and uninformed jury is just one of the reasons that I am seeking another trial in Lansing's 54-A District Court."

"So you're saying it's these issues that brought you here?"

"These issues are important. What happened to me was a total miscarriage of justice. I'm not naming any names. But listen, two deputies told me in the Ingham County Jail that I was set up and railroaded through the judicial system. The entire trial centered on whether or not the woman was able to consent to sex. It wasn't a case of rape, it was a case of race. There was tension in the administration on the first day I took office, and it was prevalent until the day I left. The alleged victim claimed to have had only had one drink with me, but several hours later, she showed up at the police station with a blood alcohol level of 0.13."

"What about the witnesses? Who were they, and how crucial was their testimony to this case?"

"After we left the restaurant, the woman was complaining that she had to use the bathroom, and we happened to be close to a house owned by one of my good friends. He rented out a property to students, and so I figured there would always be someone home. However, when we knocked on the door, I was confronted by one of the male residents. He denied us entry and told us to leave, but on the way out, I found an open door, so I let ourselves in to use the bathroom."

"Did he see you come in?"

"No, but on our way out, he spotted us."

"I bet he wasn't too happy about you coming into the house?"

"No, he wasn't. We almost came to blows. He became very aggressive, but we left before the situation escalated."

"So for how long did he and the other witnesses in the house see the alleged victim?"

"For less than two minutes."

"Was the alleged victim walking without any assistance?"

"Yes, she was."

"Then maybe the witnesses did have a motive to want to see you fall."

"There are five motions in the request for a new trial, in addition to the question of the alleged victim's alcohol consumption."

"Five motions?"

"The first is the controversy over the lie detector test that I took and passed. The prosecution submitted the test during the trial as a 'second statement.' This statement was inconsistent with the original report."

"A polygraph statement is inadmissible in court."

"That it is. The second statement taken from the polygraph was more detailed because the police asked more specific questions. I feel the judge allowed the jury to take my second statement out of context. He allowed the statement because he knew there were inconsistencies between the two. If the jury understood the circumstances surrounding each statement, they would have come to a completely different conclusion. The second factor in the motion is Judge Thomas Brown's failure to explain to the jurors that they could have remained undecided."

"At the beginning of the trial, weren't the jurors given standard instructions?"

"Yes, and in those instructions, they failed to mention or explain the concept of a hung jury."

"Didn't your lawyer try to intervene?"

"It was shocking when the judge refused to read our supplement to the jury. They may not have known that they could have come out undecided. But instead, they sent a note to the judge stating that they were having trouble coming to a decision."

"Why would he refuse to brief the jury about these issues?"

"As far as I'm concerned, the judge wanted nothing more than a conviction."

"Well, I'm a little pressed for time, but that should be enough. Thanks for your time."

"Thank you for coming out to talk to me, Maria. I want to tell my side of the story."

I watched her gather her things and waited for her to stand before I rose to my full height. I then reached out to shake her hand. She took my hand and smiled before turning away and walking out of the room. Then Deputy Red entered the room, shuffling his feet.

"Let's go, Parker—it's time."

I followed Red to my cell. A few days later, I was sitting in the recreation room after the guards had just changed the television room rules. Now they can control the remote due to a fight that broke out two days ago between two White inmates. I hunkered down in my chair watching the five-o-clock news, and to my disbelief, they only aired one minute of my interview. My tired eyes honed in on the small, thin, blond reporter holding a microphone out in the Michigan winter breeze. She shivered while speaking, and I hung on to her every word.

"Phil Parker maintains his innocence. He claims to be the victim of a high-level conspiracy. Wrapped in these claims are Judge Thomas Brown, the Department of Public Safety, Lansing police, and Ingham County prosecutor, Don Martin. Parker said he's not confident Judge Brown will go against the ruling. Instead, he wishes to take his case to the Michigan State Court of Appeals. Liz Grane here, reporting live, from the Ingham County Correctional Facility."

Photo credit: The State News (Newspaper)

CHAPTER 8

·✦✦✦✦·

Sweet Resolution

Those on work release moved to Post Seven this morning. I wanted to join them, although Deputy Red refused that idea as abruptly as it hashed. He did observe me talking to *Channel 6* yesterday. Today, three Caucasians and four African American inmates came in from Detroit. Most of them are violators. These inmates are waiting for transfer to Western Wayne on Tuesday. One of them happened to stray from the crowd. Steve is tall, burly, and he walks with a limp. I watched him sliding his rough fingertips across the knife wound on his left cheek. The uneven abrasion hid under his dark brown five-o-clock shadow.

"I'm Steve."

"I'm Phil Parker."

"I know."

"You know?"

"Yeah, Coach. Word travels fast around here. The jails are jam-packed in Detroit, so they parceled us here for now. Come Tuesday, most of us are transferring to Western Wayne. I've been in a dungeon in that place, and it's nothing nice in Detroit, man."

"Is it really that bad?"

"Bad? The thirteenth precinct was bearable, but most of my time, I was in the hole. I did two years in the pen and was supposed to be out by the first week of December. Instead, I fucking broke parole on a drug charge, and now I'm swimming up shit creek without a paddle."

"That's some tough luck. Hey, it's kind of chilly in here. Do you want some socks?"

"Thanks," he replied, accepting the offer while his teeth chattered behind that faint smile.

There was a thin line of saliva snaking down his rough, acne-scarred cheeks, and judging by those scars, there were probably much deeper ones still hidden under his clothes. I looked into his brown eyes and saw pure fear, and at that moment, I felt sorry for him. We quickly developed a very base-level friendship, and after he showered, I let him borrow some lotion. I worked out hard today, doubling my standard push-up and sit-up routines. I felt wholesome and spiritual this evening; Sellik cut the music on at 6:45 a.m. while Skinny and Ivory played cards. I tossed and turned until I couldn't take it anymore. Skinny is 6'5", bald, dark-skinned, and sinewy, whereas his counterpart, Ivory, is 5'2", light-skinned, and built like a linebacker. They are total opposites. Their voices were starting to drive me crazier by the minute.

I sprung from my bunk and found Deputy Shiek hovering in front of my cell. Edison Shiek was a bear of a man. He stood at least five inches over six feet, and this middle-aged Peruvian packed the muscle. He had a thick black mustache, thinning hair, and deep-set, dark eyes that seemed to quiver periodically. His age showed through a haggard, grimy five-o-clock shadow and leathered pale skin.

"Deputy, could you please turn on the television instead of the radio?"

"I just conducted a cell check. Why didn't you ask then, Parker? Weren't you asleep?"

"I wasn't, but the music is still on."

"Yeah, it is. Isn't it?" Shiek walked away, grinning.

He enjoyed every bit of the external power given by the Ingham County Correctional Facility. He's been particularly tough on us this week, and we've felt his wrath in various ways, including him not opening the doors and his refusal to change the television station when asked.

MILITIA JUSTICE

December 14, 1992

Stacy (also known as Country) stole his roommate's cakes and, in turn, went to lockdown. Country is morbidly obese, dark-skinned, and much shorter than your average guy. While on lockdown, he squealed on several inmates, including my friend, Ivory. I tried my best to keep to myself because tensions on the block are at an all-time high. I was awaiting my phone call, and that's all that I cared about right now. So when my time came, I was ready to let out some pent-up frustration. I stood there, holding the phone, anxiously waiting for Stuart to pick up. I just needed to talk to someone who could assure me that there was still hope.

"Phil."

"I need to talk to you, Stuart. Can you come in on Monday?"

"Yes, I think that I will. How are you holding up in there?"

"Not good. Not so good. We'll talk on Monday."

"Yes, Monday, we will meet."

"Okay," I replied, feeling somewhat relieved, and since there still was phone time left, I decided to call my sister, Lawana.

"Hey, Lawana."

"How are you doing, Phil?"

"Fine."

"Georgie's been messing up, but I still love the guy."

"Really?"

"Yeah, but I won't go back, Phil. I promise you that. Even if I have to live with a broken heart."

"Hearts mend in time. Take care of yourself, Lawana. Thanks for the call."

"We're here for you. Keep your head up."

"Bye," I said, taking in a deep breath.

Later that night, I worked out and then shot some hoops. Lt. Kady was on the row. He is tall and broad-shouldered. Kady walks with a limp, but everyone knows he's fully capable of bringing a world of pain down on any inmate stupid enough to end up on his shit list.

"You know, if it were up to me, we wouldn't go to the gym at all," Lt. Kady grunted, his blue, beady eyes now fixated on me.

"I'm glad it's not up to you then," I replied, looking him dead in the eyes, and I didn't look away until he did.

After working out, I read the *State Journal* and almost puked at first glance at the headlines.

"The Spartan wrestling program is on the rise," I read aloud.

It was appalling to think that someone else took credit for my hard work. How soon would they forget who built that team? While I was lamenting, a fight broke out between Heavy D and Manson Erving. Heavy D is light-skinned. He stands over six feet and weighs over three hundred pounds. Manson, on the contrary, is short and stocky. Italian by birth, he is rugged and rough-hewn. They were fighting in the mess hall, and *D* came out black-eyed and bloody-nosed. He was pulling out Manson's hair by the time Kady broke up the fight. After the melee, there was anger in the air, and everyone was on edge. It's below zero on this chilly Michigan winter night, and it's never felt colder behind these lonely jailhouse walls.

And somewhere in the darkness, I noticed my roommate staring at me after waking up in a cold sweat. Sneering menacingly, I made him feel my rage. After that intense moment, he never looked at me like that again. The guards woke us up at 7:00 a.m., and I immediately dropped to the floor to do my morning push-up routine. Kady interrupted me, casting his round, obese shadow across the cell.

"Parker, two visitors are here to see you."

"Okay," I replied, rising to my full height.

"Make it quick because they aren't on the list."

"Why aren't they on the list?"

"Look, Phil, I'm allowing this visit, and from here on out, we will be following protocol. So in other words, make it snappy and don't push your luck." Kady was beardless with boyish good looks, but he had let himself go many years ago.

I grunted while following his lead to the visitation area, took a seat behind the glass, and found myself looking back at two of my former Michigan State wrestlers. Roy Hall and Jamie Richardson were sitting in front of me, offering their support. Jamie was holding the phone, nodding his head, and before closing his eyes, he reached out with his other hand and then placed it on the glass. Jamie was wearing his green Spartan hat twisted to the back, a white T-shirt, and blue jeans. His black hair had grown down to his shoulders, and he had two silver hoops dangling from his pointy earlobes—Roy was clean-cut and dressed in a gray warm-up suit.

"How are you doing, Phil?"

"Good. I wanted to thank you guys for coming down to see me."

"We know that you didn't do it. It's a bunch of bull if you ask me!" Jamie groaned.

"I know, Jamie. But don't worry, my lawyers are working on the appeal."

"I was just offered an assistant coaching job at Oliver, and Roy here is transferring to Western Michigan. We don't want to be Spartans anymore without you. It's just not the same. It just doesn't feel right anymore."

"That's great, Jamie. I'm happy for you and Roy. You guys are the best. I've already been to the desert. I will come out of this with wisdom, knowledge, and a new sense of strength."

I worked out, won two five-on-five games, and then went to a success seminar taught by Alan Meul from LLC. Alan looked like a computer nerd, yet he spoke like a dictator. He had bright-red hair and hordes of freckles sprinkled across his face. He emphasized the importance of learning to read and write. After the workshop concluded, I called Stuart.

"Phil, how are you?"

"I'm putting one foot in front of the other. I wanted to talk to you about a few things, though."

"What's up?"

"It concerns my visits. My brother, Sam, came from Chicago to see me, and his visit was denied."

"Denied?"

"They told him that he wasn't on the list and therefore he was denied visitation. And on top of that, I'm not receiving my mail anymore."

"Don't worry, Phil, I will talk to Major Carpenter. Call me back on Saturday to discuss the issue further."

I held the phone against my ear, waiting for the dial tone.

"You done, Parker?" Deputy Shiek asked with hate in his eyes.

"Wait, I want to make one more call."

"All right, make it short and sweet," Shiek replied.

I reached out, dialing the numbers. I anxiously listened. I was hoping for my old friend, Art, to answer the call.

"Hey, Phil."

"How's life on the outside, Art?"

"It's good, *P*. How are you doing, my brother?"

"I'm doing, I guess."

"It's good to hear your voice, Phil. I will be down to visit you soon."

"All right, buddy, talk to you later."

"Right on."

I gave the phone to Shiek, trying to avoid eye contact with the watchful and dubious troublemaker. On the walk back to the block, I noticed Pat standing over Steve at the end of the hall. Steve was scowling, and Pat was acting more reserved than usual. It seemed as if Steve's youth and aggression were finally getting the best of the older man. Pat Pinkerton is tall, thin, and maniacal. His salt-and-pepper gray hair is always clean-cut and sharp at the edges. Pat has a bad habit of standing too close to people, and if he even sensed that he was making others uncomfortable, he would merely goad them on. Steve jumped up, and before anyone knew it, they were face-to-face.

"I ain't gay, Pat!"

"Shut your mouth!"

"I will kill you if you don't get away from me right now!"

Pat silently backed away, keeping eye contact with Steve all the while. I could feel the temperature rising as they snarled at each other. I felt sorry for Pat; still, we all knew he had it coming for a long time. I wanted to intervene, but the conflict seemed to resolve on its own. And just before I reached the door of my cell, Deputy Anders cornered me.

"We need to talk to you for a minute, Phil."

The tall, lanky deputy led me down the hall and into a cold interrogation room, where Deputy Ratliff was waiting, resting his elbows on a circular table.

"Take a seat," Ratliff grunted, pointing to the empty chair. "So, Phil, we called you in to talk about Ivory. I hear he's been stealing cakes, and it would help us greatly if you could tell us what you know."

Ratliff cocked over me with bloodshot, piercing blue eyes, his trigger finger itching at his belt. His silvery hair dampened with pomade and sweat shined under the overhead lights. The much older man steadily closed the distance between us, snarling under his breath all the while.

"I will not supply you with any information to charge the brother. So if you're looking for a snitch, then you best look elsewhere."

"So you're telling me that you know nothing of these accusations?"

"I'm telling you that those accusations are no more than rumors as far as I'm concerned. And how dare you think any different."

"You'd better watch yourself, Parker."

"Huh," I grunted, making my way out of the room.

At that moment, I finally stopped worrying because I knew right then and there that one day, I would be free of the lies. I promised myself never to stop fighting.

Later that night, I was sitting with Steve. Steve Whitson was one of the few White inmates that regularly congregated with Blacks. He was a large man with dark-brown eyes and high cheekbones. He turned and looked into my eyes.

"So, Phil, can I ask you something?

"Yeah, go ahead."

"What is your position on interracial dating?"

"Well, Steve, when I graduated from college, I wanted to know the why of things. So I started developing a philosophy I call 'Superman All the Time.' You've heard of Superman. Well, even this amazing hero, with powers unrivaled by mortal men, is also a part-time Clark Kent. And in an instant, he's just another clumsy, weak-looking, and ordinary guy. And the moment he becomes Superman, he is again unstoppable. My philosophy challenges us never to take off our capes. We must root out the kryptonite and overcome our weaknesses. I feel we all need to strive for complete self-esteem and confidence. A Black person doesn't choose to be Black, nor does a White person decide to be White, but who's to say how or whom we love? We are all linked by sameness. The truth is we are all only human."

Suddenly, we were interrupted by some commotion transpiring a few cells down the hall as another fight broke out between Manson and Heavy D. D was approximately 6'4", and he sported a flattop-style haircut. He was of Puerto

Rican descent, and he had long legs and a round belly. They were fighting in the shower. *D*, battered and bloodied, was still gripping Manson's neck while four burly White officers wrestled them apart. I watched *D* hobble into his cell, feeling sorry for both of the poor saps.

I found myself trying to figure out how I felt about my new roommate, Shane. Shane's the guy everyone is talking about because of his shoot-out with the police. Two officers shot out his windows and hit him twice in the shoulder. He looks like your average tall, skinny Caucasian with dirty blond hair and a French cut, pencil-thin mustache, but make no mistake, this guy is a ticking time bomb. He never seemed to be at ease, so I just left him alone. A guy that's never comfortable in his skin is sometimes the most unpredictable type. I stretched out in my cell and then went into the television room, hoping to watch the news but soon found myself staring at a blank screen. I looked to Deputy Sellik, and he was standing at the foot of the room holding the remote.

"The television will be cut off for the next two hours since Jan from Detroit stole a food tray today," he announced with one hand on his gun belt and the other on our precious remote.

CHAPTER 9

No Way Out

December 15, 1992

Deputy Davis is on again, and tensions are at an all-time high. I flagged him down in the hallway. Dorian Davis was tall and light-skinned. His almond-shaped, dark-brown eyes were slightly upturned at the corners.

"Davis, can I speak with you, please?"

"What is it, Phil?"

"There's a snitch in my room, and I need action."

"Don't worry, Phil. I will handle it. That's my job." Davis paused, his attention shifting to shouting voices in the hallway.

"Uh-oh," I grunted.

"Looks like Rob and Chi are fighting over the mop," Davis said, rushing into the crowd of inmates.

Chi and Rob stood chest to chest in the middle of the mob. Rob's wild blond hair was wet and unkempt, and he had this look in his green eyes as if he had gone completely insane.

Chi was kneading a pick through his knotty Afro and blatantly refusing to give an inch.

"You don't talk to me like that, Robert!"

"My name is Rob. Don't you dare call me Robert," Rob snarled, reaching out for the mop.

Before they could get a hold of each other, Deputy Davis managed to position himself between the two.

"Settle down, fun's over. Everyone needs to go back to their cells, or I will lock this motherfucker down right now!" Davis shouted before drawing his baton.

Jasper had returned to Post One. Jasper is the quiet type, yet everyone knew not to mess with him. The silent ones are always the killers. I cornered him in the hall.

"What happened to Peanut?" I asked while looking into those emotionless, brown eyes.

"Word on the block is that he transferred out. They said he was sick of seeing intellectual movies in place of cartoons."

"I applaud him for that."

"Yeah, y'all were always at odds over the television."

"Well, not anymore, I guess," I said, turning and walking the other way.

And just as I had turned the corner, I ran straight into the new kid on the block, a short, slightly rough-looking White boy with the nose and ears of a wrestler.

"Hey, aren't you the Spartan wrestling coach?"

"No. Former."

"I'm Bill Avita Jr."

"Are you related to Bill Avita, the national champion?"

"Yes, sir. He's my dad."

"Wow, it's a small world," I mumbled, before continuing on my way down those all too familiar, pale prison hallways.

Later that evening, I made one more attempt to call Stuart. When he didn't answer, I went back to my cell, wondering if I had made a mistake in trusting him to handle my appeal. Restlessly, I lay down on my cot, staring up at the ceiling until the lights went out. On the surface, I may look calm and collected, but deep down, I am slowly losing patience on another dreary Michigan night.

December 16, 1992

I was off today on the basketball court. We lost three games to two, but overall, recreation time was fun. A man will go crazy when cooped up in a cell all the time. As time winded down, Sheriff Wigglesworth came shuffling into the gym. Wigglesworth was short, bald, and obese. I didn't know why he was there since Claude Thomas' son was working the second shift. Suddenly, an intense communication session between Jerry, Freddie, Rob, and Steven erupted in the gym corner. Jerry was downing Rob because he was so effusive about his self-help concept of the world, another one of his lists of crazy world concepts. Jerry seemed to tower over Rob. Rob just kept on running a black fist comb through his long, silky, black hair and looking the other way while Jerry raged. Jerry had these dark canine-like eyes, and his skin was course and ashen. Freddie stood out like a sore thumb. It must have been his pale complexion and bright fire engine-red hair that made him so bizarre looking. He strayed on the outskirts of the commotion, watching intently. Everyone's kind of edgy right now, and I feel that we might be on the verge of a race riot. By 11:30 p.m., my new roommate stumbled into the cell. He's boney, White, and young.

"I'm Phil," I said, throwing my arms over my head.

"I'm Jimmy Potts. Nice to meet you," he replied.

"So what are you in for, Jimmy?"

"They hit me with five days for driving without a license."

"Don't worry, kid, you'll be out of this place in no time."

Jimmy dropped to his bed and fell fast asleep while I started doing push-ups. I pushed myself until my arms went numb. Then drenched in sweat, I continued pumping the reps, thinking of my family, my career, and my reputation, when suddenly I was abruptly interrupted by the shadow of Deputy Davis. I stood up facing the handsome young brother, and I knew that he was a good man with one glance into his eyes.

"Hey, Phil, take it easy," Davis mumbled.

"It feels good to let it out."

"I don't want you having a heart attack on me. You're too heavy to carry down to the infirmary."

"Sometimes, the pain just feels good. It's a release, I guess. In here, we don't have many freedoms."

"That's true. Hey, I heard what happened between you and Bemis."

"He wouldn't allow me a razor in the morning."

"Well, he said you were late to respond to the call."

"Then at 6:25 a.m., I requested my drops, but the sleepy dope claimed to have done a medicine call earlier. I told Bemis that I didn't want to quarrel over timestamps. I go by the doctor's orders, not by his."

"I will talk to him. I'm working a double shift today, and to be honest, I'm not in the best mood."

"It's just another day in paradise."

"I didn't see you at breakfast time, Parker."

"That's because I'm fasting today."

"Really?"

"Yes, sir."

"You hang in there, Phil."

"I will."

I completed my workout with doorknob grabs and push-ups and then went into the TV room. The minute I arrived, Heavy D's arguing with Steve 'The Biker' over the remote. Steve Jameson joined various biker gangs throughout his youth and now the chain-smoking, over-weight Irishmen's past was catching up with him. He was broken nosed and haggard.

"You ain't interrupting *Tom and Jerry*, I don't care what you say," Steve said, clenching his fists while face-to-face with Heavy D.

"Everyone here wants to see Atlanta play Detroit, so back down right now, old man," *D* replied, clenching his fists.

D looked like he wanted to break Steve's face, but sometimes you just need to let it go.

December 17, 1992

I just came off a week of fasting today, so I need to eat to build my strength. Ten inmates from Post One came in this morning with the Detroit parolees. The dorm is too full, and tensions are at an all-time high right now. I noticed a fat, dark-skinned brother with a long, scruffy beard trying to take over the TV in the foyer. He's new in our dorm, and he intends to dominate. He is trying to intimidate me, but I shut that down immediately.

"Say, man, we wanna watch *60 Minutes*," I said, looking into the brown-eyed brother's eyes.

"I'm watching *Ghost Dad* right now, old man."

"Who the hell do you think you are?"

"I'm Ron Neal, remember that name, and Big Ron just don't give a damn."

"I don't care what your name is. Behind these walls, the majority rules, and the majority wishes to watch *60 Minutes*."

I reached out for the remote, and Neal jerked back, holding it tight.

"Don't ever touch my hand!" Ron yelled.

"You don't intimidate me one bit," I shot back as Deputy Red intervened.

"Let's take a vote, with a show of hands, everyone that wants to watch *60 Minutes* speak now or forever hold your peace," Deputy Red implored the group with one hand on his baton all the while. Then Red paused, watching the crowd, and counting the show of hands.

"Now, who wants to continue watching *Ghost Dad*?"

When only a few inmates sided with Ron Neal, the decision was clear.

"Okay, *R*, hand it over," Deputy Red grunted, standing over Ron.

Neal grunted, reluctantly changing the channel.

"Phil, Dewitt wants to see you in his office. Come with me," Red said, pointing at me.

He led me down the corridor to the last office on the left. Dewitt was waiting patiently at his desk.

"Sit down, Phil," Dewitt said, pointing to the chair on the other side of his desk.

Dewitt has a medium build, a round face, and judging by his salt-and-pepper gray hair is probably in his mid-forties.

Red nervously left the room, closing the door behind him.

"I watched the trial. They allowed the girl to perjure herself. She lied about the amount of alcohol she consumed and the prosecution, judge, jury, and the police only encouraged those lies," he said in a low tone.

"I was caught in a web, a web of injustice. There was no justice coming from nowhere."

"They wanted to get you out of there, and this was their only chance."

"Who are they?"

"I can't name any names, but just know that there are people in your corner. Keep on fighting, Phil."

"I will."

"We will talk more another time. I just wanted to let you know that I know."

"Thanks, Dewitt," I said before being escorted back to my cell by Deputy Red.

December 18, 1992

This morning, I woke up feeling uneasy. I stretched, and I watched a *Maury Povich* episode about Jeffrey Dahmer. Fat Boy was eyeing me the whole time. I stood my ground and let him know with one look that I wasn't putting up with any crap today. Fat Boy stood six feet four. The young man's broad shouldered, middle-aged, African American, and mean as hell. He liked to use his heavy frame as a tool to intimidate most, but I'm not the least bit afraid of Willard Jackson. As far as I was concerned, he's just another chump. After watching TV, I read letters from Landon, Ann, Peggy, and Judy. Several hours later, I worked out, and before I knew it, the day had turned into night. Time is flying quickly, and I wasn't even counting the days anymore. Tonight's deputy, McGuire, is one of the worst of the worst, and I can hear his squeaky voice screaming from down the hall. McGuire was a short Irishman with bright-red hair and freckles.

"You have five minutes to lock down, or it'll be forty-eight hours lost. One minute to go!" Thomas McGuire announced as he continued on a tirade.

And throughout the dorm, they're whispering words of complete disdain for his aristocratic, insensitive commands. Voices are stirring in the darkness, and some are talking revolution. It is store order night, and static's coming from all four dorms.

"Okay, that's it," McGuire lamented, his voice is becoming louder and more abrasive. "There will be no more store orders," he officially declared, pacing up and down the hall, causing more inmates to cry out. "Blasphemy!" inmates are shouting, and at that moment, I felt as if we were on the verge of complete chaos. I clenched my fists as if preparing for a fight, and after a moment of uneasy silence, he spoke again.

"Okay, I'll give your asses one more chance. And if you don't cool it, I'll pass them out at 3:30 a.m.!" his voice rose above the din. Then a few minutes later, my name is called.

"Phil Parker, room 14," McGuire said in a low tone.

I looked for him at mealtime, but he's too intimidated to come out with me to the food court, I suppose because of his racist, belligerent attitude. The following day, I'm awakened by the sound of screaming. Someone out there was being brutalized. I arose from my bunk, stretched out, and went to work out. Jasper was doing push-ups in the hallway. He jumped up when I passed by him.

"Parker," his voice stopped me in my tracks.

"McGuire is a racist. He threw my store order at me today."

"Really? He threw it, huh?"

"Yeah, he threw it. He's a snake and peckerwood."

"He's not the only one," Jasper chuckled while I continued to the gym.

I worked out like a maniac today, pushing myself until I couldn't even feel the reps anymore. I was thinking about what Dewitt told me the whole time. Was it a conspiracy? Are Stuart and the judge involved? The more I thought about it, the more I felt entangled in a white web of injustice.

Several inmates were shipped out to Post Four today. Word on the block is their transfers are due to their classification as sex offenders. I wrote a kite to the jail administrator and then slipped it to Deputy Davis in a sealed envelope. I let him read a duplicate copy in front of old Eugene Ryan, the tall, skinny food cart attendant. After reading my letter, Deputy Red looked into the logbook to find my medical file.

"It's not here," he muttered, and under his breath, there was a hint of menthol cigarettes and cheap whiskey.

He kept rummaging through the files and then placed his hands on his hips, shaking his head in frustration.

"This is unusual. I will check on it," he grunted.

"Don't even worry about it at this juncture," I replied.

The whole thing was beginning to reek of foul play.

December 19, 1992

Today, I picked up the paper, and lo and behold, Grady Peninger is making headlines. Peninger built another hall of fame honor, and in his statement, he claims to be now working with the MSU program. Everything was starting to fall into place. Grady was still in his office throughout my whole tenure at Michigan State. What was he doing there? My enemies were always lurking around me. They set up camp, learned my ways, and then set me up. They sent Jane to me. Maybe they paid her to do it, or perhaps she's just a pawn in this conspiracy. What was in it for her? Was it money? Some people would do anything for the right price. Who was this young girl who so quickly went from sweet to hateful, from salacious to cold, from lover to accuser? Today, I've been transferred down the hall. This place was built to house the worst of the worst. Jasper, from Detroit, is my new roommate. His knotty hair is now tinted brown, and a deep scar stretches across his right cheekbone.

I am still thankful for being in a medium-security lockdown facility. I've come to grips with my closest perception of what it is like to be in jail, and even though I'm behind these bars, I won't let them make me a prisoner. I am now in a dorm that consists of twelve. Each room has its day to control the TV or radio, and our day is on Thursday. I quickly realized that cleaning the dorm in the morning is the way to be rewarded. By midafternoon, I called Atty. Richard Amburg and found myself shaking with excitement.

"Hello, Mr. Amburg, I'm Phil Parker. I was referred to you by my good friend, Judy Becker."

"Phil, I've been awaiting your call. First, tell me about Stuart's appeal issues. I know that he's looking to move forward with this appeal as soon as possible. However, I'm not too impressed with his effort. A polygraph is admissible in the motion for a new trial, if not the trial itself. You should check and see if Stuart knows this."

"Are you telling me, the top lawyer in Ingham County doesn't know how to do his job?"

"No, apparently, that's what you're telling me. Listen to yourself. Try to put two and two together. I'm going to need a police report and transcript. You can request this info from Stuart.

And, Phil, to retain my services, it's going to cost you five thousand."

"My financial statement has been submitted."

"Well, it must be approved by the state before we are to move forward with this."

"I guess so."

"Well, I hope to talk to you soon, Phil."

I hung up the phone and just sat there deep in thought. It was hard to imagine that some of those smiling faces, so close to me during this ordeal, were untrustworthy. I then called Stuart.

"Phil."

"Stuart, I need to ask you an important question."

"What is it? Have you received the transcript yet?"

"I have the appeal on the basis that the evidence wasn't there to convict. After the paperwork goes through, you'll get the transcripts."

"Oh, I see. I'll get back to you, Phil. I gotta run."

The guard met me in the hallway.

"Hey, Parker."

"Huh?" I turned to mumble under my breath.

"There's a woman here to see you," Davis said in a muffled tone.

I followed him to the visiting area and then found myself staring through the glass at a somewhat frazzled-looking Judy Becker. She's dressed in a red turtleneck sweater, blue jeans, and a pair of black clogs.

"Phil, how are you holding up, honey?"

"Okay," I replied, trying my best to smile, but it just didn't feel right.

"You don't look so good."

"I know. It must be the food."

We laughed for a moment and then our eyes met. Judy must have sensed that I'm beginning to lose hope.

"Phil, you're not gonna believe this."

"What?"

"On my way back from a gathering in Howell, I slid into a ditch. It took a tractor to pull me out of it."

"Wow, good thing you weren't injured. That's what we need to be thankful for."

December 31, 1992

Today is the last day of 1992, and what a year it was. Adjusting to life in jail is an everyday struggle. I wrote to Peggy today about my conversation with Pitts and Amburg. I know she'll be impressed by this new development. Amburg wants 7,500 if we plan to continue with his firm. It was noisy as ever last night. The Lone Mexican in Dorm *C*, Chavez, and his roommate, Black John, were carrying on, acting like complete fools till at least three in the morning. Black John was a dark-eyed, swarthy young man with a toned muscular frame. I have to admit that Chavez is one hell of an artist. I found him sketching the faces of various inmates in the mess hall one day, and it was fascinating how he captured their distinct features and peculiar mannerisms. A few knuckleheads in Dorm *C* kept the radio on the whole time that Deputy Sellik was patrolling. It's so hard right now, but I will just try to take it one day at a time. I know that in the future, I'll be back with my family. One day, I will be free again.

January 1, 1993

It's the first day of the New Year. I got up at nine forty-five in the morning, ate Rice Krispies for breakfast, and stretched out with the new guy, Timmy, from Flint. Timmy is a needle neck redheaded, seventeen-year-old White boy with a temper like a hair trigger and a chin shaped like a crescent moon. Timmy and Stoney from Eaton Rapids are inseparable on this block. Stoney, Italian by birth, grew up in Lansing. He was a stocky man with a florid face and a long puritanical nose. After doing some push-ups and sit-ups, I watched the Bulls play the Pistons, and while staring at the television, my thoughts were fading elsewhere. I'm in a daze, thinking about my family, the verdict, and my shattered career. To believe, in an instant, I had lost everything. However, my release date is steadily approaching, and that calms me. With every passing day, I'm gaining hope, and hope is the light that inspires me to never ever give up.

Today, Michigan State and Oklahoma State faced each other in a dual wrestling meet, and Oklahoma won twenty-three to thirteen. I read the article shaking my head the whole time. There's constant noise around me, and I'm on the verge of snapping. I kept it together for my family. They're my motivation. I can't let them down by yielding to the rage inside. I learned a long time ago that sometimes it's just not worth it. Bruce Miller, the Vietnam veteran, is up writing on the table next to mine. I sat down beside him because I desperately needed to talk, and Bruce made me feel comfortable. I wanted to let out some steam, and Bruce was one of the few inmates that could put me at ease. He's burly, well-muscled, and not the least bit afraid to say whatever he thinks. He has a full head of light-brown hair and keeps a full, scruffy beard riddled with streaks of gray at the tips.

"So what are you in for, Bruce?"

"Huh?" Bruce dropped his pen, and we locked eyes for a moment.

"You don't look like you belong here."

"Cocaine—I'm here on cocaine charges. They found two pounds in the trunk of my blue sedan."

"Wow. Where are you from?"

"I'm from Boise, Idaho."

"There's no place like home."

"It never feels like home in this fucking hellhole."

"If a home is where you hang your hat, then I don't want to hang my hat here."

"So what's your story, Phil?"

"I don't want to go into it. Believe me, these walls have eyes and ears."

"You're the ex-head coach of the Michigan State wrestling team, the one accused of date rape. I followed your trial. I followed the testimony, and I will tell you right now, Phil, I expected the verdict in reverse."

"You and me both. I was railroaded."

"It was a trap."

"A trap?"

"Yeah, Phil. They set the trap, and you fell right in it."

"Well, I'm a week away from a motion for a new trial. So at this point, I'm looking to break free from that trap."

"That's the ticket."

"One day, justice will prevail," I avowed, rising to my full height, and, after breathing a deep sigh of relief, continued on my way back to my cell.

Later that night, I wrote to Peggy, Landon, Ann, and broadcast news legend, Ed Bradley.

January 2, 1993

I awoke in a cold sweat, experiencing stinging pain shooting down my left hip. I stretched out and then wrote a kite to the medical department regarding a request for a new mattress. I made sure to give the letter to Deputy Davis, and I kept a copy for myself. While in my cell, I read a letter from my beautiful, devoted wife, Peggy. She's my angel and my strength. It was the only letter I hadn't read yet. She wrote about her family in California, about Landon's problems at school, and of Ann's inability to make new friends; still, altogether, her letter assured me that my family had been unbroken by the injustice of militia justice. She also informed me that she had contacted the *Donahue Show* concerning my case. After reading her letter, I opened a package sent from my eldest brother, Sam. It was a copy of *Nick and the Cyclones*.

"Wow, those were the days," I whispered, staring blankly into the darkness, reminiscing.

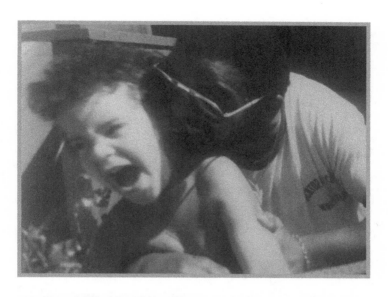

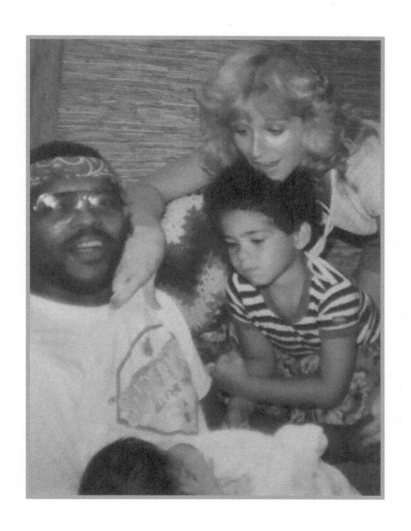

From 1972: Iowa State heavyweight Chris Taylor, right, with wrestling teammates, from left, Ben Peterson, Phil Parker and Carl Adams before facing Drake University.

The Des Moines Register (Article by, Cody Goodwin… "Carl Adams, former Iowa NCAA National Champion, to be inducted into National Wrestling Hall of Fame.")

CHAPTER 10

The Way Home

Word on the block is three White supremacists are now in custody. The men held are accused of burning a Black man. The deputy's rotation changed tonight, and I caught Deputy Okin in our room. I just happened to wake up, and to my surprise, the squirrelly, pasty White, middle-aged, redheaded deputy was scrambling around.

Incensed, I tried my best to rest, but I ended up just tossing and turning all night in my sleep due to a hip injury. I found a moment's relief from the pain when thinking of the book, *Black Rage, White Justice*, which is scheduled to arrive any day now. My oldest sister Terry sent it a long time ago. At this point, I am counting down the days until it's here. I just needed something to get my mind off what was happening in this lonely life behind the walls. I've been taking Tylenol for my hip injury, and it's left me feeling slightly dizzy.

On the way to the recreation room, Slap confronted me about the TV again. I felt someone approaching me from behind. When I turned around, Slap clenched his fists and entered my personal space, a place where most dared not to tread.

"Parker, you don't own the TV. I'll pull the plug so that no one can watch it. Now, how about that!" he said, towering over me.

Slap's approximately 6'5", and his chiseled features and deep-set eyes showed traces of West African roots. Beads of sweat rolled down his dark skin as tempers flared to a boiling point.

I moved forward, staring at the younger man with my heart pounding. I could feel the blood pumping through my veins.

"That's a no-no," I replied.

At this point, I was clenching my fists and preparing to pounce.

"I'm not afraid of you. Just because you're a world-class wrestler, doesn't mean you can fade me!"

"I'm not afraid of you just because you're an inmate. That doesn't mean you can fade me!" I replied, carefully keeping my feet planted.

Slap is a tank of a man. He's one of the most prominent African American inmates in the Ingham County Correctional Facility. There was pure rage trapped in those dark-brown eyes, but I'm confident had this conflict turned violent, I would be the one coming out on top.

"Let's get it on!" Slap shouted, kicking the chair over.

"Let's do it!" I replied with outstretched arms and no fear in my heart.

Deputy Davis then jumped between us. "You guys better calm down. Break it up before I put you all on lockdown."

"It's all right, I won't stoop to his level," I grunted, walking the other way.

I'll let him get away with it this time, but if he ever touches me, it's over for him.

Snow came down harder than usual yesterday, and today I've decided to stay inside. We've had to endure life without hot water for two days. The knuckleheads on the block are awake and looking for trouble. Slap and Todd cleaned this morning, and they were making a racket the whole time. I struggled with anxiety and depression tonight. I was looking at pictures of my family, and it must have been the sparkle in their eyes that led me to a dark place. I felt like I had let them down. Aside from the fact that the judicial system railroaded me, I had committed an offense against my family. Peggy is willing to look past my mistakes, but I wondered if my kids could be so forgiving. I vowed right then and there that I would make it right with them before I closed my eyes and fell asleep.

January 10, 1993

I'm watching *Maury Povich*; the theme of this episode is the Mike Tyson trial. Alan Dershowitz is asking for a new trial. The judge and prosecutor can censure the trial and allow what evidence they want. If both parties are lying, then he'll be acquitted. A few hours later, I am in Room 39 with Bruce and Chris playing cards. Chris is 5'8", stocky, and clean-cut. Beasley, the new deputy on the block, called a cell check around eight forty-five in the morning. It was within minutes of the last inspection, so I felt he made the call in error.

"Cell check," I said loudly enough for him to have heard me.

"Everyone in, except room thirty-nine!" he shouted back in a very abrasive tone.

"Cell check," I said again, this time louder than before.

I went into my room, and he came barging in, red-faced and snarling. I took one look at the fresh-faced, middle-aged, ex-garbage collector and found myself feeling sorry for him. He's not cut out for this type of work, and the other inmates knew it. His military-style bald fade and deep abrasive voice didn't fool any of us for a second. We all knew that he was softer than a pillow. He's tall and built, but behind all those muscles, I sensed fear.

"When I say something, you're going to do it. Do you understand?" he barked.

"Yes," I said.

"I'm not in the mood for your belligerence. I can move you somewhere else. I can move you somewhere that you don't want to be. You understand me, Parker?"

"Yes," I replied, watching him walk away.

At this point, I'm shaking with anger.

"Don't even worry about him, Phil," Jasper said, dangling his feet over the bottom bunk. He's lying casually on his back with his arms folded under his head.

"That punk wouldn't even last one minute if it went down."

"I know, Phil, but you need to play it cool, man. Your release date is coming up, and you don't wanna mess that up for anyone, brother."

"You're right. I don't need to prove anything to him."

"Right on, now you're talking my language. You don't belong here, Phil. And we all know that. They know it too!"

"You mean the guards?"

"Yeah, man, they know you got a bum rap. So for the time being, follow their rules. Just play their game for a little bit. And before you even know it, you'll be out of here. You'll be free as a bird."

"I don't know."

"Why do you say that?"

"Because when I get out of here, a new battle begins."

"And what battle is that, Phil?"

"The battle to prove my innocence."

The next day, I ran into Sellik in the hallway. He had this look on his face like he wanted to kill me. His right eye was twitching while we stared each other down, and the closer he got, the angrier I became.

"Where's my paper?" I asked in a low tone.

"Your paper?" he snarled back.

"Yeah, my *USA Today* newspaper."

"It hasn't come yet?"

"Well, could you call and check?"

"If it isn't there, it isn't there," he replied, moving closer, holding onto his nightstick.

I knew he wanted to send me to the hole, and I was determined not to give him a reason. Then suddenly, Bruce Miller stepped in. Bruce is a mild-mannered, reasonable guy with brownish-blond hair and a medium build. He's doing time for domestic abuse, and it seemed he is learning from his hardships to be a better human being. Bruce walked me to the foyer. We waited for a few awkward moments and then he looked at me and spoke in a low tone.

"What's the problem, Phil?" Bruce asked.

"He's got his mind set on bringing me down. But it does not happen."

And while we waited for a transfer to transport us, Deputy Shiek was approaching us from behind.

"Here's your paper Phil," Shiek grunted, handing me the most recent edition of the *USA Today* newspaper.

"Thanks," I replied, feeling somewhat surprised at their prompt response to my request.

"Don't take it into class with you, bald head."

"Okay, no problem. And by the way, your head is balder than mine, so don't throw rocks from a glass house."

Shiek's face suddenly turned red, and I sensed he is on the verge of a breakdown.

"You'd better watch your mouth, Parker. One more bad word from you, and I'm gonna send you to solitary!"

This was the second time he had threatened me in one day, and I am beginning to see right through the empty threats. The shower had been too cold for the last two days to even bear for more than a few painful minutes, and my hip isn't feeling any little better. I was limping through the days but wasn't feeling the stinging pain shooting down my leg anymore. I laid on the top bunk, being careful not to wake up Jasper, and when I closed my eyes, I could hear his voice whispering.

"So what's up with you and Sellik, Phil?"

"He's a chump. That's all."

"He's watching you, man. You need to be careful."

"He's withholding my mail. I still haven't received the book my sister, Terry, sent over two weeks ago."

"I, too, haven't received a book that a friend of mine sent two weeks ago."

"This is as discriminatory as it gets, Jasper."

"You're right, Phil. And that's why we need to stick together. Don't let him get you off track. You're going to be out of here soon. So don't let them delay your release."

January 11, 1993

I worked out for the first time since Wednesday. It felt euphoric to work, sweat, and push my body to its limit. I sincerely needed this release. After working out, I trimmed my beard a little lower than usual. A part of me longed to start fresh with a clean slate. Sellik is on again. I will use every effort to avoid him. I'm fasting today, so I was slightly agitated while following Deputy Shiek's lead down the hallway to the phones.

"Keep it short and sweet, Parker," Shiek said, handing me the phone.

I dialed seven digits as if by rote and held the phone against my ear, waiting for Stuart to pick up.

"Hello," his secretary's voice was unusually raspy this midafternoon.

"Hi, this is Phil Parker, one of Mr. Dunning's clients. Is he available?"

"No, he just left for court. Can I take a message?"

"Yes. Let him know to get in touch with me ASAP."

"Okay, I will."

"Thanks," I replied, shaking my head.

I was concerned Stuart had made no contact while Deputy Shiek led me to the mailroom, where Sellik was waiting. He moved toward me, keeping his fingertips fixed on his gun belt.

"Loosen up, Parker," Sellik said, folding his arms over his chest.

"Loosen up?"

"Yeah."

"Okay," I replied, even though I didn't mean it.

Sellik seemed to want to make peace with me, so I humbly obliged.

"Just keep it cool, Parker. Don't make it harder than it has to be," he said, reaching out with his free hand.

I took his hand and let our feud go right then and there. After getting my mail, I went to lie down, and at approximately one in the afternoon, Sellik informed me that my lawyer was there. He led me to the visitation area, and while I'm gathering my thoughts, Stuart was waiting for me, dressed in a blue suit, and there was a hint of exhaustion in his eyes.

"Here's a copy of the motion I just filed," he said, handing me a stack of paperwork.

I sat down and took a few moments to examine the fine print. I was carefully reading between the lines, and the more I read, the more I saw errors. It is becoming evident that the transcripts were altered.

"There are two obvious errors here, one being that you put second-degree criminal sexual assault instead of third-degree criminal sexual assault. The other is your fourth reason for requesting a new trial should have 'insufficient' instead of 'sufficient' evidence."

"I will correct that. This is just a rough draft, Phil. Also, I wanted to inform you that we're not going to court tomorrow."

"Why's that?"

"I looked up the admissibility of the polygraph results in the motion and found that in the case of the *People v. Barber*, you can only use it in conjunction with new evidence. So I want to talk to the person that had given me the info a little bit more before we explore our options."

"I can't believe this," I grunted, feeling taken aback by the fact that Stuart waited until the day before we were to file the motion to come to this decision.

I felt infuriated, sitting across from the man that would be representing me in the fight for my freedom. I wanted my life back, and I now questioned if Stuart is really on my side.

"Both Peggy and I are interested in exoneration. Please don't take this personally, but we need your best possible effort in this appeal. My career is on the line here. To put it plain and simple, I need your best."

"Okay, I understand."

"Do you, Stuart?"

"I'm gonna try to set the motion date for February."

"Did you consult your father or an appeal attorney about this?"

"No, there's no such thing as an appeal attorney.'

"You know what I'm saying, like Dershowitz for Tyson. I'm serious in this go-around." I stood up, and we shook hands.

"We will check on the transcripts. Call me on Friday at ten thirty," Stuart muttered before we parted ways.

January 12, 1993

Kady starts the first shift. Kady was tall, beardless, and rough looking. The product of two Russian immigrants, he knew the value of hard work all too well. Jasper made a motion to change the TV policy. He stood up in the recreation room with outstretched arms, scowling at all of us.

"Instead of room to room, let's vote, and the majority rules," Jasper announced.

It was eminent that dissent was coming from Todd and Chris.

"If we do change, then we win," I said, hoping to reiterate Jasper's point.

Later that evening, I finished a stress seminar. It was very enlightening. We did visual imagery relaxation and then practiced breathing techniques. The focus of the discussion was on productive ways to cope with stress. After the class, I went to the phone and called my sister, Terry.

"Hello."

"Hey, Terry."

"How are you doing, Phil?"

"All right, I guess. But you know, I'm just taking it one day at a time. It's rough in here—real rough."

"I know it's tough, but you're tough too. You're one of the toughest guys I know."

"Thanks, *T*."

"No, I really mean it. And tough times don't last, Phil, tough people do."

"You're absolutely right, sis."

"They returned the book I sent to you. So I guess they're calling it contraband."

"That's completely ridiculous. This dilemma is the simplest case of cruel and unusual punishment. I mean, come on! It's a fucking paperback!"

"It's just outrageous, Phil."

"How are Mom and Dad?"

"Well, Dad just got admitted to the hospital for a blood clot in his leg. Mom said his leg was turning green."

"I wish I were there to talk to him and see him."

"Stay strong, Phil. You stay cool in there."

"Okay. I will, Terry."

I hung up the phone and walked back to the block, feeling like I was moving through a foggy gauntlet. I felt powerless and locked in a cage. Life was happening outside these walls, and here I missed birthdays, holidays, and celebrations. Here there were no genuine smiles, only expressionless faces and frustration. Hate is everywhere, and at this point, I'm just counting the days until my release. A new inmate just arrived in Room 39. He's tall, Mexican, and meaner than a rabid junkyard dog.

"What's your name, man?" I asked, approaching his cell with caution.

"Rodriguez," he grunted, lying on his back and running a pick through his long, greasy black hair.

I looked down at his arms, sleeved with tattooed faces of beautiful Hispanic women. He has brown skin, a wide jaw, and the black eyes of a killer.

January 13, 1993

Lansing's about seven inches thick in snow, and today, the scent of blood is in the air. All the news stations are talking war with Iraq. Jasper is pacing the cell, looking distressed, and I'm lying on the top bunk, thinking about my family.

"What's wrong, Jasper?" I asked while jumping off the cot.

"Things are falling apart for me right now, Phil."

"What happened?"

"I observed on the computer today that a bench warrant has been requested for me by my probation officer."

"What's that about?"

"I didn't come back in time, and they caught me drinking. So I had Kady check the computer, and he came right back with the news. Sgt. Sheldon's handling the case."

"Oh, you mean the short, vivacious brunette?"

"Yeah, she's my probation officer. This is all bad, man."

"What's the issue?"

"They know I violated the rules, and they're going to extend my jail time."

"Damn! And you're only four months to your release date!"

"I don't wanna have to tell my wife about this, Phil!"

"Try to put things into perspective. Wait until the end of January before you do anything. Let's not alert anyone until then."

"Yeah, Phil, you're right. I'll wait," Jasper said before collapsing on his bed.

"I'm going to work out. You coming out?"

"No, I'm staying in."

"Okay, suit yourself," I replied, stepping out into the hallway.

Rodriguez leaves today. He chose to spend his last day watching TV with Bouee. I passed by him on the way to the phones. Still sore from my

morning workout, my thoughts were fading elsewhere. I outdid myself this time, doing push-up
after push-up, and before I even knew it, I had
pumped seventy-five reps. I dusted myself off
and then bulled through the line for the phones.
Choking on the unpleasant aroma of cigarettes
and cheap cologne, I called Mom and Dad. And
there, leaning against the wall, I found myself
imagining how great it would be to be with them
right now in Chicago.

"Hello," my mom's voice chimed in.

"How are you, Mom?"

"Phil! What a pleasant surprise! I was just
thinking about you."

"How are you doing?"

"I'm good, but your dad isn't doing too
great. The blood clot has traveled from his leg to
his lung. They did surgery on him yesterday and
inserted a device from his groin to his heart. It
will go through the artery to expand it."

"I'm shocked. I can't believe Dad is in serious condition. This is surreal!"

"Don't you fret, son. Jackie's gonna be just
fine. I prayed all night, and I know he will heal. I
just know it, Phil. He will have to take medicine
for the rest of his life, but believe me, son, he's
gonna be around for a long time. He ain't going
anywhere. How are you holding up in there?"

"I'm fine. You sound so strong and composed. I admire you for that, Mom. You're the
strongest woman I know."

"I get my strength from God."

"Well, Momma, you hang in there."

"I love you, baby. Hold on, wait just a second. Sam wanted to say something to you."

There's a brief moment of silence before Sam is on the phone.

"Hey, bro."

"Phil, what's the good word?"

"It's your world, Sam. I'm just living in it."

"I wanted to tell you. They returned the articles I sent you."

"Not at any time was I notified about anything returned."

"I sent you the results of the Midlands tournament that took place on Wednesday."

"Well, keep everything as evidence, and I'll notify my lawyer about this."

"You hang in there, bro."

"I will, Sam. Take care and tell everyone that I love them."

"You are always in our prayers, Phil."

I hung up the phone and then proceeded back to the block, dragging my feet against the floor. My hip is bothering me again, and I could feel sharp pains shooting down my leg with every step.

The lights are dimmer than usual in the recreation area. Shannon, Todd, and Jasper have taken over one of the circular tables in a horde for their daily card game; and of course, they are cheating again, and others are starting to catch on to it. I took a seat, and, within minutes, I was invited to join the game. Shannon is a bear of a man. He's always wearing a white T-shirt that's freshly clean and pressed. Todd is short in stature yet walks around carrying 195 pounds of pure muscle. He's a redneck from head to toe. His countenance kept going from blank to irate as tensions rose.

"You're kind of little, aren't you?" Jasper said, locking his cynical gaze in Todd's direction.

Without making eye contact with anyone, Jasper pulled a big joker from his deck of cards and then slammed it upon the table, laughing hysterically.

"Ain't nobody gonna mess with me. I'll kill you. I might be small, but I'll kill you!" Todd barked, standing up and shoving the chairs to the side.

Todd recently shaved his head and was looking like a different person. Jasper met him in the foyer, and now they were standing face-to-face. Todd stood his ground with clenched fists and trembling lips. After a few tense moments, Shannon moved in between them.

"Y'all need to cool off. We're trying to play cards here, and no one's going to interrupt my game," Shannon proclaimed, pushing the two men aside.

Todd and Jasper went in opposite directions before the guards rushed into the foyer. Officer Sellik is leading the pack of three overmuscled, angry, White "good old boys."

"What's going on in here?" Sellik inquired, his eyes looking in every direction.

"Nothing's happening. It's just a little card game argument. Things are settling down. Everything's cool," Shannon replied.

A few hours later, I found myself dozing off while watching *The Maury Povich Show*. This episode centered on what happened in Rosewood, Florida, seventy years ago on the day when hundreds of African Americans were massacred. It all began when several angry Whites formed a vigilante posse and went looking for a Black man who allegedly raped a White woman. Minnie Lee Langley's a living testament to the climate of racism that commonly existed during the pre-civil rights movement. Minnie remembered the execution of her father.

"He was forced to dig his own grave and then shot in the head," she recalled with no trace of tears in those dark-brown eyes, yet her hands were trembling when she spoke of him; and I knew at once that this loss still haunted her.

She had tubes in her nose, helping her breathe out, but still looked elegant sitting there in a wide-brimmed, white sun hat and a flowing, flowery, pink dress. I felt a chill of greatness and encouragement travel down my spine as I strolled to the phones, putting one foot in front of the other.

By the time I reached the phone, the line had dwindled to just two inmates. While standing there, I thought about my beautiful, loving wife, Peggy. She's my rock and strength. There's no one quite like Peggy. Every time I open my eyes to those pale prison walls, I find myself counting the days until we reunite. I reached out for the phone and then called my parents.

"Hey, Phil."

"Hey, Mom. How's Dad doing?"

"Dad should be coming home tomorrow. He'll be receiving home care for the next few months."

"Well, tell him to hang in there. We love him, and we're all praying for him."

CHAPTER 11

Wallowing in Darkness

January 14, 1993

Today is Bill Clinton's inauguration. I heard the first click of the door and shot up to my feet. Clinton's attending the service at a Black church, and this is the first time any US president has participated at a Black church. The great Frederick Douglas was a part of this church. Benny, the youngest inmate in the dorm, is treading a fine line. He's blond, skinny, and timid. It's his day to control the TV, and he insisted on watching *Sesame Street,* but I talked him out of it. After watching the local news and the sports broadcast, I made my way to the phones and dialed Stuart's number.

"Hey, Phil."

"Stuart, I wanted to inquire about the transcript request."

"I spoke to Teresa Gallegos, and she hasn't finished the transcripts yet."

"She's still trying to complete the transcripts for the DNA trial? I don't understand why she can't give a specific date."

"Has your lawyer mentioned any knowledge of the polygraph issue?"

"I thought we were on the same team, Stuart."

"We most definitely are. It's up to you, man. I'm here if you need me."

"We must be diligent in our efforts if we wish to overturn the decision. Honestly, I think that if we go back to court for a second trial, we'll surely win."

"Well, it's a process, Phil. Let's take it one step at a time."

"All right, we will."

"Call me tomorrow morning so we can talk some more, Phil."

"Will do," I said, hanging up the phone and continuing on my way to the block.

I turned into the TV room, and Jasper stood in the front, attempting to call a meeting.

"Did y'all know two inmates were sent to ICU today for injuries sustained in a fight over the TV? We need to change the rules because they're not working," Jasper said, pacing before the group of seated agitated roommates.

A hush swept through the room and then only quiet whispering.

"Majority rule is fair, and fair is fair!" Brent grunted, angrily ripping the cable out of the socket.

Brent White is only 5'7" but stocky and well-muscled. His sandy blond hair held a few traces of gray wisps. He was a former Hell's Angels biker with a short fuse and wild, brown eyes. Nobody crosses Brent, but he didn't intimidate me at all. Instead, Brent's face reddened while he let his emotions overrule better judgment. He picked up a table and moved it aggressively toward Jasper.

"You better sit back down, peckerwood!" Jasper warned, clenching his fists and squaring his feet.

Then Don from Detroit stepped in Brent's path. Don is tall, dark-skinned, and ten years older than Brent. Brent is wearing a white T-shirt and house slippers. We all braced ourselves as Brent lifted the table in the air. This gesture of disrespect sent Don lunging forward. Don mustered his anger and threw the right hook that left a trail of blood trickling down Brent's right cheekbone. Brent then dropped the table and retreated out of the room, holding his jaw. Suddenly, Deputy Sellik barged in. After the commotion had settled, Don and Brent were put on twenty-four-hour lockdown. Twenty minutes later, Sellik came back to finalize the policy.

"Majority rules still stand here," Sellik declared, panting for breath.

The next day, I found myself sitting across from Claude Thomas. He's wearing a red shirt, a black tie, and two shiny-looking black dress shoes. I rested my elbows on the table, anxiously waiting for him to speak.

"Phil, I wanted to let you know that it takes time to get transcripts. But just because it may take some time doesn't mean that I'm not 100 percent here for you."

"Do you think Brown will grant us a new trial?"

"Maybe, due to the polygraph discrepancies. If he feels it warrants one, then I'm confident that he will."

"Well, if he's able to do so, then I will also retain you for my civil case against Michigan State University."

"Let's just take it one step at a time, Phil."

I left our meeting feeling somewhat confident in Claude. Claude Thomas is one of the top lawyers in Lansing, and he knows how to play the part. Still, while traversing down the dimly lit aisles, I reflected on my days as a wrestling coach and realized that it was all over. It was unsettling to feel stripped of my rights, good name, and freedom. Jasper was leaning against the wall as I turned the corner, smiling.

"What are you so darn happy about, Jasper?"

"I'm not gonna be in here any longer than I have to."

"What about your parole violation?"

"I got ninety days in a drug and alcohol residency program."

"Hey, that's better than jail."

"Any place is better than jail, Phil."

"See, things don't always turn out as bad as you thought they would."

"No, they don't. Watch yourself, Phil. Sellik is on again."

"I'm on my way to the gym. We'll talk later."

"See you later. And, Phil?"

"What?" I stopped in my tracks and then turned to face him, noting the tears now welling in his brown eyes.

"Thanks for your words of encouragement. I won't ever forget who helped me through those dark times," Jasper said, his countenance devoid of emotion.

"No problem," I replied before continuing on my way to the gym.

And the whole time, I could feel the heat resonating from eyes watching me in every direction. It's a jungle in here, and to survive, I had to unleash the animal in myself. It's basketball day, and there was a violent game of three on three going on as I stepped into the gym.

Sellik reached out, touching my shoulder from behind. "I see you looking at the doors. Don't get any bright ideas about escaping, Parker."

"I'm gonna find my way out of here the legal way," I replied, moving on my way.

I can hear Shannon and Bouee talking about me in the hallway to Jasper.

"Coach disrespected me!" Shannon said in a booming tone.

"Cool out, man," Jasper intoned.

"He's old enough to be my dad. Fuck Coach!" Bouee's raspy voice mouthed the words as I casually walked past him, looking him dead in the eyes the whole while.

I had to continually remind myself to refrain from violence because here, violence only breeds more violence. In thinking about Judy's conversation with Jane, I realized that we should use this as new evidence in conjunction with the polygraph.

"Hey, Phil," Jasper called out. I could hear his footsteps trailing mine.

"What's up?"

"Don't even worry about it, man. They're just blowing off some steam."

"I'm not the least bit worried about them."

"I'm a little concerned about something else."

"What's up?"

"I haven't talked to my wife in twenty-four hours. It's so unlike her not to call."

"Keep calling. Try not to jump to any conclusions."

"You're right, man. I'll keep calling."

"Don't give up hope, Jasper. Don't ever give up hope."

"And, Phil, there's good news for you."

"What is it?"

"I heard through the grapevine that Shannon is being transferred soon."

"That's good news for him and me."

"Why's that, Phil?"

"'Cause the boy was about to be ragtagged."

"He's a troublemaker."

"That, he is. Well, I'm exhausted, man. So I'm checking in for the night."

"I hear you, Coach."

I left Jasper standing in the hallway and continued down the aisle toward my room. Despite being surrounded by jailhouse walls, freedom was getting closer, and I could almost taste it in the cold, thin air.

January 15, 1993

Today, Shannon was transferred to Dorm Eight. I could hear fights breaking out as I rolled off my bunk. I paced about the room, trying to make out what was going on, and as I looked out into the hallway, I watched Lt. Vissar, Deputy Yeager, and Johnstone rushing into Dorm *C*. Lt. Vissar was ruddy and obtuse. He had black hair and brown eyes. Johnstone was short, stocky, and brazen as they come. And Deputy Yeager was raw boned and very loquacious. Five minutes later, they put us all on lockdown. *A* and *D* was locked down for twenty minutes while *B* and *C* was on twenty-four-hour lockdown.

By 6:00 p.m., you could feel the tension in the air. I heard Jasper and Todd arguing in the hallway, and when I left my room, they were standing face-to-face. Todd was looking like a madman. His eyes were bloodshot red, and a thick mustache is covering his lips.

"Your old ass can't deal with me. You better watch it!" he shouted, turning his attention toward me.

"I bet you ain't gonna mess with me," I then shot back, stepping in between them.

Todd clenched his fists, and at that moment, I knew he was about to swing. I reached for his wrists, and before he even knew it, I had him deep in a full-nelson hold.

January 16, 1993

I exercised harder than ever today. I could feel beads of sweat pouring down my skin as I continued to push myself way past the limit. My muscles were numb to the pain as I did push-up after push-up, letting out the rage. Kady is on today. I could hear several inmates crying out. I guess one needs to scream one million times to get the old kook to break the doors. Kady's one of the most experienced guards in the block. The other guards look to him for validation. He stands approximately 6'4" and walks around at 245 pounds most of the time. He came to my door with a look on his face like he wanted to kill me.

"Mr. Thomas is here to see you."

"Good," I grunted, feeling optimistic, steadily trailing his steps with my head held high.

Kady led me to the visiting area, where I soon found myself sitting across from the dapper, middle-aged African American young man dressed in a pinstripe blue suit and a light-blue silk shirt to match. He reeks of exotic cologne, and there's a trace of arrogance in those light-brown eyes. I placed the phone against my ear and then touched my fist against the glass. He met my gesture with his fist pressed against the other side. His voice is deep, calming, and soothing to the ear.

"I want to take over your case with MSU, Phil. That's why I'm here. If you win this appeal, then we need to come in with our guns blazing."

"That's what I'm talking about."

"I'm gonna do some legwork regarding your criminal trial and then I'll get in touch with Stuart to arrange a conference with the department."

"That sounds like music to my ears right now."

"I've done my homework and familiarized myself with your philosophy."

"I see."

"I know about your 'Superman All the Time' approach to life."

"Well, I believe that one must never take off their capes. Even Superman is a part-time Clark Kent. Clark's the part of him that's ordinary when in contrast, his alter ego, Superman's the exact opposite. Now, imagine Superman, a hero capable of incredible feats without Clark Kent. Imagine a Superman immune to kryptonite."

"I love that, Phil. All the time."

"It's all the time, brother."

"And this situation will work itself out in due time."

"Thanks, man. I needed to hear some good news right now."

"Be a rock, Phil. Don't let this destroy you. You can come out of this a better individual."

January 17, 1993

I awoke to the sound of Deputy Faust's reverberating voice.

"I wanna know which one of you assholes thinks he can get away with taking laundry bags! No one will rest until the culprit comes forward!" he yelled, going room to room, frantically searching for a trace of evidence.

His tirade finally ended at Anthony's cell. Frankie Faust is a middle-aged, dark-haired Kentucky boy. Supercilious, arrogant, and overbearing, Faust took every opportunity to humiliate us. Anthony's the quiet type. The boy rarely even says a word to anyone. Anthony's a former football player with a chip on his shoulder. He's young, light-skinned, and always ready to fight.

I made my way to the door and watched them take Anthony out of the cell in handcuffs. He had this look on his face like he just didn't care anymore. Then Deputy Thomas and Dewitt came in to remove Bill Falls from the dorm twenty minutes later. Dewitt had thinning black hair and bushy eyebrows. He was shrewd, wrinkled, and tight-lipped around the other guards.

When they brought Anthony out of his room, he was shirtless, and his brown, wavy hair was wild and unkempt. His eyes were bloodshot red, and he's pointing in my direction.

"Fuck you, Coach. This is your fault. I'll see you on the outside!" he yelled as they carted him out.

I guess he felt that I was responsible for his removal, but honestly, I had nothing to do with it. I never snitched on anyone.

January 18, 1993

Todd took an instant liking to his new roommate, Garth. Garth's a Purdue graduate, in here for embezzlement. He makes it quite apparent that his two daughters are the most precious people in his life. Garth Rouble's one of the most hated inmates because he hardly showers and likes to sleep the days away half of the time.

An older man named Heiger came in today as Bouee's roommate. He's six feet tall, and his movements are slow and labored. While watching TV, I noticed him nodding off. Todd didn't come out for dinner on time, so Deputy Thomas left him locked up for a while, and by the time Thomas let him out of his cell, his face was beet red.

"Fuck you, Thomas! You can't lock me in like that!" Todd yelled, pounding his fists against his chest.

While making my way back to the room, Clark "the Cripple" stopped me in the aisle. Clark's skinny, and he walks with a limp due to an old football injury. He was a barber on the outside, so he kept his gray hair freshly lined up.

"Hey Phil, let me get your cake!"

"No, man," I replied, brushing right past him.

It seems like these guys are always trying to take something from you, and cakes are like gold here. I hear it's only thirteen degrees outside, and behind these walls, it feels at least ten degrees colder.

Deputy Thomas stopped me right before I got to my room. "Here, Phil," he said, handing me a copy of the amended motion for a new trial.

There was no stamp on the envelope, so I wondered how it got here. Stuart had to have come in and left it, but why wouldn't he contact me first? Why would he do this? I was feeling mistrust toward my lawyer. I found myself sitting across from Stuart the next day, staring back at him through the plate glass. He's well dressed, as usual, looking dapper in his navy-blue suit and matching navy-blue dress shirt; but his tie is wrinkled at the folds, and his hair is knotty and matted. I held the phone against my ear, making a point to look into his eyes. He looked like he hadn't slept in days, and there was a thin, white film building around his lips.

"Phil, how are you holding up?"

"I'm just taking it one day at a time."

"They've delayed your trial to have the polygraphist come in and testify. So I will motion for a new trial based on the miscarriage of justice where Brown allowed the jury to take your second statement out of context."

"Sounds like a plan."

"When are you gonna sell your house, Phil?"

"Soon enough, I just need to talk to Peggy. It's hard to do anything while locked up in here."

"I know. Just stay on top of things, and I will do the rest."

"I will."

"Take care, Phil," Stuart said, rising to his feet.

I remained seated for a moment, and while watching him walk away, I noticed a dip in his hip and a slide in his stride that wasn't there before. Was he really for me? Or was he just playing me? I was beginning to wonder. It now was all coming together, like pieces of a puzzle. Maybe one of my main problems was the counsel I chose to defend me. He wanted money, power, and respect, but did he care about right and wrong? Did he care about justice? Did he care about the truth anymore?

I reluctantly got up and made my way down the hall. It's depressing in here at times. It felt like the walls were closing in on me. When I got back to my room, I overheard Aaron hassling Ben. Aaron's 5'2" but built like a bodybuilder. The guy always has a chip on his shoulder and rarely ever smiles. He keeps his hair in tight cornrow braids, and he has a black heart underneath his right eye. Ben is a young dark-skinned brother, who looks out of shape, but what he lacks in physical conditioning, he makes up for in heart. He is known to fight at the drop of a hat, but for some reason, he wasn't taking up for himself in this particular instance. Both dorms hovered around the windows while Aaron continued his tirade.

"C'mon, punk! What you gonna do?" Aaron continued, following Ben down the hall with his arms outstretched.

Ben just kept walking and staring blankly ahead. It was as if he's in a daze. Maybe he's now giving up or giving in. Either way, he's showing weakness, and in here, that was a dangerous thing to do.

January 19, 1993

Brian Kaus is on today, and when he did a morning cell check, I could hear him huffing and puffing.

"Hell of a combination," Kaus grunted while sneering at Jasper and me.

Kaus was chubby, rubicund, and powerfully proportioned. He assumed that we were asleep, yet minutes after he left, Jasper got up from his bunk and turned toward me. I was lying casually on my back, staring up at the ceiling.

"Did you hear that?" he asked in a low tone.

"I sure did. What do you think he meant, Jasper?"

"He doesn't like me."

"I guess he feels the same way about me."

"Don't worry about him. All we have to do is serve our time and make it out in one piece. It doesn't matter what he says!"

"You're right, Jas! He's not worth it!" I rolled out of bed, feeling a stinging sensation shooting down my leg.

"You all right, Phil?"

"Yeah, I'm cool. It's just my hip acting up again."

"Well, take it easy, man."

"I will be fine," I replied as the door opened.

"You coming out?" Sellik asked, peeking in.

"No," Jasper replied.

"What about you, Phil?"

"Yes, I'm coming."

The door opened, and I limped out into the aisle.

"You all right?" Sellik inquired with a smirk spreading across his face.

144

"Yeah, I'm cool."

"Where are you off to today?"

"I'm going to get a haircut."

"Let's go," Sellik said, leading me to the barber chair where Heavy D was waiting with his clippers in hand.

"Hey Phil, today you are in luck. I just finished Todd off, so I guess you're next," Heavy D snickered under his breath while brushing excess hair off the chair.

I felt better after the cut.

Later that day at recreation, we won two basketball games in a row. I just couldn't miss a shot. By midafternoon, dressed in the county orange jumpsuit, I called Berna from the *State News*.

"Hey, Berna."

"How's it going, Phil?"

"It's going. Please survey judges and lawyers on their opinion of my appeal. I want to know if the issues for a new trial are valid enough without having to go to the appellate level."

"That's possible. Maybe I could pull a few strings to make it happen."

"I had a conversation with an independent lawyer on Monday."

"Who's the lawyer?"

"Claude Thomas."

"I will speak to the editor about doing a survey."

"Sounds good."

"Hey, I want to come out there with my photographer to do an interview."

"That'll be fine. I will send you the motion hearing document."

"Okay, Phil. See soon."

"See you then."

I set the phone back on the receiver, feeling confident in my appeal. This is my chance to turn it all around. And I couldn't wait to make the wrongs right. When I got back to my cell, Jasper was pacing the room.

"What's wrong, my brother?" I asked.

"Sellik's a fucking racist. I heard him say that Blacks have no rights."

"Well, we sure don't have too many rights in here."

"You ain't lying about that, Phil."

Suddenly, deputy Kaus came to the door.

"Phil!" he called out.

"Yes," I replied, moving to the door.

"I need to talk to you," Kaus grunted.

"What is it?" I answered, stepping out into the hallway.

"I heard you're looking to meet with the *State News*."

"Yeah, that's true."

"So you're ready to tell your story, huh?"

"I guess I am."

"We will be talking to you soon."

"Whatever," I grunted as the sound of shouting voices that drew his attention elsewhere, and somewhere in the darkness, a fight was breaking out between Whites and Blacks in Dorm *C*.

Fifteen minutes later, the whole dorm shut down. Bruce met me in the hallway, panting and wearing a surprised expression on his face. Blood was leaking from his torn orange jumpsuit, and his underarms were soaked with sweat.

"Hey Phil, you were just on the radio and television."

"Really?"

"I didn't realize what a big deal your case is around here."

"I just want justice, that's all."

"Well, maybe you just might get it," he replied, running his finger across the peach fuzz of his cleft chin.

Today is recreation day, and I desperately needed to work out. I proceeded to the gym, and when I got there, we played three basketball games and lost every single one. The gym director took a basketball to the face, courtesy of Fred Newman. Newman is a bear of a man but has the IQ of a seventh grader. Fred was one of the loudest White inmates in Dorm *C*, and his red hair made him stick out like a sore thumb. Bob, the director, was down for a while, writhing in pain. Bob Trent was a witless, balding, older man from Wales. I was asked to stay with him. I prepared a bag of ice and held it on his face until help arrived. Nurse Buckle quickly came to his aid. Sharon Buckle hurried her fleshy, impish frame to the scene. She was a shrewd woman with narrow hips, a thin nose, and shoulder-length silver hair.

"Why are you putting plastic to his skin?" she barked.

I was shocked that she somehow could find fault in my attempt to help. I was fully aware that she didn't know what she was talking about, so I kept quiet. She wrapped up his wounds and told the director that she'd tend to him later. When I got back to the dorm, Bouee and Todd were continuously parroting my name. It's getting ridiculous. I wish they would knock it off. Then Deputy Dewitt cut the radio off all night. Maybe now, I can finally enjoy a decent night's rest.

Several inmates are leaving tomorrow, so things are quieting down, and it is colder than ever in my room. I could hear the sounds of footsteps pattering as I tossed and turned throughout the night, drowning in my nightmares all the while.

CHAPTER 12

One Last Stand

January 20, 1993

Sonny is one of my favorite fellow inmates. He is 6'4" and 245 pounds of manhood personified. His broad shoulders and barrel-like forearms kept the bullies at bay most of the time, but I've seen him tested on a few occasions. He's leaving today, and I've never seen him look happier.

I found myself longing for tomorrow while exercising in my cell. This place has been without heat for two weeks, and it's only getting colder behind these walls. Some inmates in Dorms *B* and *C* are walking around with blankets wrapped around them. This is cruel and unusual punishment, and it feels like there's no justice coming from nowhere.

This morning, I picked up the *State News* and read that MSU wrestling had won two matches against Central Michigan in bold black ink, but they failed to print how they got dry-waxed by Minnesota. Ironically, the results of the match were in the statistics department.

However, they didn't want to admit that the program's not headed in the right direction.

Jasper and Moss are up. Moss, built like a tank and dark-skinned, was a like a parental figure on this block. His shoulder-length dreadlocks often swayed past his short, handsome face and gray eyes. Several inmates will be free men this evening, so I've been walking on eggshells all day. First, I attended church, hoping to rid myself of the crippling weight of disappointment. The minister, Paul Garrett, was inspirational. He sang and played the piano, and for a moment, I felt like I was free again. I closed my eyes, and I could almost feel the wind touching my skin. After church, I made my way to the phone, looking to talk to my mother.

"Hey, Mom."

"I'm so glad you called, Phil. You really made my day."

"Hearing your voice is comforting."

"Thank you, baby."

"How's Daddy doing?"

"Your father's doing just fine. He and Terry will be celebrating their birthdays on Wednesday."

"I miss you all so much."

"We miss you and love you, Phil. It's not right what they've done to you, but you must trust in God. He will help you pull through this trying time."

"I will, Mom. But you know, sometimes it feels like no one cares anymore about the truth."

"They care. When the facts are presented, they will care. So keep believing, Phil."

"I will. I love you all."

"We love you too, Phil."

I hung up the phone, fighting back the tears. I wanted to break down at that moment but managed to hold the emotions back. I couldn't show the other inmates any sign of weakness. Around here, fear and intimidation reign. After talking to Momma, I dialed my wife. Peggy answered on the first ring.

"Phil, what a pleasant surprise." Her kind voice warmed my heart.

"Hey Peg, how are the kids."

"Ann's great, but Landon's having a hard time."

"What's wrong?"

"He says he wants to live with Mary and attend school in California."

"Why is that?"

"He's not getting along with the new crowd, and he doesn't want to go to school anymore because he feels like everyone is against him."

"He needs to be careful of the danger."

"Yes, he does."

"Well, I will call you on Wednesday night."

"Okay, Phil. I love you."

"I love you too, Peg."

"You stay strong."

"I will."

"We know that you're innocent. So don't ever forget that."

"I won't."

"We're always here for you."

"Thanks, Peg."

"Talk to you soon."

"Later," I muttered, resting the phone on the receiver.

I hear voices whispering all around me. I took a deep breath, then reached out, picked up the phone, and dialed Stuart.

"Hey, Phil."

"How's it going?"

"Not too good. I'm battling a touch of the flu."

"I wanted to let you know *Channel 10* is coming in on Tuesday to interview me."

"You contacted them?"

"No, they contacted me. Why, is there something wrong with me talking to the press?"

"Well, I just think you should have run it by me before coming to this decision."

"I can't keep quiet anymore."

"I don't think it's the best idea, Phil."

"I wanted to see if I could be delayed for the transport out for the interview."

"You probably have to leave an order to do that."

"Well, can you call and check for me?"

"I guess. Do you have the money for the polygraphist?"

"Yes, I do. And I wanted to let you know that I hired Claude Thomas for my case against Michigan State University."

"What happened to Art?"

"Let's just say we had a conflict of interest."

"Okay."

"Claude will be attending a hearing for me on Wednesday because we want to get on the ground level as to what's happening."

"He's not gonna counsel this, is he?"

"No, I guess not."

"Remember how the press got involved and distorted everything last time? I don't think the media's on our side. I've got to go, Phil."

"Later," I mumbled, feeling distant from him and his ideals.

I wondered whose side he was on. Was he for me, or did he have ulterior motives? I wrestled with these questions while eating chopped barbeque pork and potatoes for dinner. It wasn't nearly as good as it looked on the plate.

Deputy Stoney was on. He's one of the youngest African American guards in the Ingham County Correctional Facility. He approached me in the hallway as I made my way back to the cell. There was an awkward look on his clean-shaven, youthful face. I sensed he wanted to ask me something, but for a few moments, he just stared into my eyes, and I made it a point not to look away or look down. He reminded me of myself when I was his age. He's short in stature and well-muscled.

"Phil, I heard you did an interview."

"Yes, I'm working with the media to gain attention for my appeal."

"No one around here could even believe the verdict, everyone thinks you got railroaded, Parker."

"That's what happened."

"*The State News* is coming tomorrow morning to interview you."

"I'm ready for them."

"Well, good luck."

"Your words are worth more than gold to me, my friend. I appreciate the support."

"Hey, the truth is evident that Jane Snow wasn't raped. She never said there was a struggle. Heck, she only testified to having one drink!"

"And don't forget, after I dropped her off, she went barhopping and binge drinking. That doesn't sound like someone too intoxicated to move her hands."

"I hear you, Phil. Just keep fighting. And don't ever give up!"

"I won't."

"No matter how hard they try to break you down, don't ever forget the truth!"

"The truth will set me free!"

"That it will, my friend."

"See you on the flip side."

"Get a good night's rest tonight, Phil."

"I will try," I muttered, making my way back to the room, and for a brief second, almost forgot about being incarcerated.

At that moment, I felt free again. Free as a bird. Free as the wind. My feet were weightless, and chills ran down my spine. These dark halls weren't closing in on me anymore. On this night, I had hope. On this night, I was on the road to redemption.

I lay down on my bunk that night, thinking about my son, daughter, and my wife before going to sleep. A few hours later, I awoke to the voice of Sgt. Greensfield. Though new to the dorm, he's a veteran of the Ingham County Correctional Facility. Greensfield's been working in Chicago for a year, and he recently transferred back to Ingham County, where he had worked for eleven years. He is tall, middle-aged, muscular, and Irish to the bone. His stern face is usually clean-shaven, and he has chiseled features and heavy bags under those piercing blue eyes. Only sixty days is between him from retirement, and it seemed he was getting more brazen by the minute. He led me to the library, where reporter, Natalie Barna, and acclaimed photographer, Reggie Johnson, awaited my arrival. I was both surprised and relieved to see a Black photographer with her. Natalie's a short, bubbly middle-aged woman. I couldn't stop admiring her long, silky black hair. She's wearing a purple blouse, black slacks, and black clogs. I sat down, eager to touch all areas of the case.

"So, Phil, do you mind if we tape our interview?" Natalie asked.

"No, that'll be just fine," I replied, peering into her enchanting green eyes.

"So, Phil, how did we get here?"

"Racism, the injustice of the judicial system, and racial relations."

"What about this alleged rape?"

"Well, I believe the whole thing was a setup."

"A setup?"

"Racism is the meat. Michigan State University has great potential, but certain elements are preventing it from reaching this potential."

"Certain elements?"

"For example, Grady Peninger, the former MSU wrestling coach, remained in his office throughout most of my tenure. Grady was a known racist. He hated seeing me succeed."

"Really?"

"He would always be talking about me behind my back, and people would tell me some of the things he would say about my family and me."

"So how does he tie into all of this?"

"He called my wife a platinum blonde when, in reality, she was a true blond. The guy didn't like the idea of me being in an interracial relationship. I honestly believe he was out to destroy me from the very beginning."

"I still don't see how he could be involved in all this."

"Well, he remained on the outskirts. That is until I hired Dan Severn. Dan was a Bobby Douglas referral, and he was trouble from the beginning. He got to know my ways, and I would sometimes go out to have a drink here and there on road trips. You see, I am a married man, but my wife and I had sort of an open relationship."

"Did she see other people?"

"No, but she looked the other way when I did. I guess she understood how I was from the beginning. When we got married, I told her I wasn't ready for a completely committed relationship, and she agreed to work with me."

"So she didn't mind you having extramarital affairs?"

"Well, let's just say she put up with it."

"That didn't create a damper in your relationship?"

"We didn't let it come between us. My wife was diagnosed with Crohn's disease at twenty-four, and as time progressed, her health was slowly failing. She wanted me to be happy, and I know it wasn't right. But I guess it was my folly. If I could go back, I would've changed. I would've remained faithful to Peggy. It was my weakness, it was my greatest weakness. But there's a big difference between cheating on your wife and rape. I'm here for rape. And that's a crime I did not commit."

"So I'm still trying to figure out how your former assistant coach, Dan Severn, and Grady Peninger are possibly involved in this."

"I fired Dan as my assistant coach and, within months, made this crucial mistake."

"Go on."

"He was pocketing meal money and slandering me behind my back. So by the last week of December, I fired him. Then subsequently, Jane Snow walks into my life."

"What is her connection to Dan Severn?"

"Well, I believe that Dan contacted Grady, and Grady Peninger rented property to Jane's brother. It was Jane's brother who accompanied Jane at the police station when she initially accused me of date rape."

"Wow, what a coincidence. I don't know if I can print this. I'll have to do some research. But if what you say is true, this is either a major coincidence or a great conspiracy."

"That's what it was. It was a setup. Jane said in court that her dream was to become a stripper."

"Wow, that's an interesting theory."

"Ultimately, it was the judicial system that let me down."

"How do you feel about your chances with this appeal?"

"I feel confident, and after I win the appeal, I plan to pursue a civil lawsuit against Michigan State University."

"I enjoyed talking to you today, Phil. Do you mind if we get a quick picture?"

"No problem," I said, posing for the photographer, looking into the camera while Reggie took a few snapshots.

"Thank you, Phil. Good luck with your appeal," she said with a hint of a smile.

"Thank you for meeting with me," I replied, watching them walk out of the library.

Greensfield led me back into the hallway, and today I was feeling more confident than I had in a while.

"I had them deliver a hamburger to your cell since you missed lunch," Greensfield said, patting me on the shoulder.

After the interview, I made my way to the phones, looking to call Claude Thomas. I quickly moved through the line of agitated inmates, and within minutes, I was eagerly dialing numbers and holding the phone against my ear.

"Hey, Phil."

"Claude, what's going on?"

"You tell me."

"I wanted to talk about my transport on Wednesday. Stuart told me that the transport was automatic, and he didn't need to request my presence. He also wants to check on *Channel 10*'s interview, set to air on Wednesday at 9:30 a.m. So there should be no conflict with your transport."

"Well, Phil, I've been looking into your case, and I saw George's affidavit. It was both good and bad. I looked at the accusation made by Kathy Lindahl at the Washington Airport."

"Kathy, the assistant athletic director? She's a bigot."

"Do you think she has something against you?"

"I don't know."

"I'll be out there to visit you tomorrow."

"Sounds good. Well, it's almost that time, so I gotta go."

"I hear you. We'll talk soon."

I exercised in my cell, doing my daily routine of push-ups and sit-ups. I felt particularly anxious this morning to find out if the *State News* had run my story today. We had recreation, but a few minutes into our three-on-three basketball game, Kady takes me out to meet with Claude Thomas. Deputy Kady led me to the visitation area, where Claude was waiting on the other side of the glass. He was dressed to impress, in a neatly pressed brown suit, beige shirt, brown shoes, and brown socks to match.

"Hey, Phil, how are you holding up?"

"I'm doing all right."

"I've confirmed the interview with *Channel 10* at nine thirty in the morning tomorrow. I will be there."

"Great."

"And Phil, I ran into Stuart, and he told me he would be relieved when his case goes to an appellate court."

"Wow, I'm not overly surprised but slightly disappointed that he was reluctant to divulge this."

"I will tell you more at a later time because I gotta run."

We parted ways, and I was feeling confident about the hearing tomorrow. Claude Thomas and Stuart Dunnings III ran my defense on both ends, and I felt like I had all bases covered. I spent the rest of the evening playing cards with Jasper, Heavy *D*, and Bouee. Tomorrow's my court date, and I was trying to keep my mind away from the stress of it all.

January 21, 1993

Today is court day, and I am up stretching at 6:00 a.m. when Jasper walked into the room with some disturbing news.

"Phil, I heard that you're going out on the morning transport instead of the afternoon."

"Who told you that?"

"Bradley."

"No way," I immediately went into the hall and found Bradley standing in the aisle, leaning against the wall.

Bradley's tall, dark, and ugly. He has deep scars stretching across his cheeks and horrible razor bumps lining the back of his neck.

"What's wrong, Phil? You look like you saw a ghost," Bradley said.

"I just heard that I'd be going out in this morning's transport instead of the afternoon."

"Yeah, that's what Sellik said this morning."

"Can I call my lawyer?"

"You can call him from receiving at six fifteen," he replied.

A few minutes later, Kady led me to transport.

"Can I call my lawyer now?" I asked, trailing his steps.

"Court takes precedence over an interview!"

"Well, you need to call *Channel 10* and notify them," I shot back.

But he wasn't listening anymore. I was then placed in a holding cell with thirty other inmates waiting to go out. It was loud and somewhat putrid. The air permeated with body odor, and I could hardly breathe. A homeless inmate with no socks had his feet up, and they were reeking.

Standing just a few feet away, a freckled inmate with bright-red hair is pacing back and forth and chanting in a singing tone.

"Murderer, murderer, murderer," he sang, and his raspy voice was breaking the whole time.

Mike Carrol is his name, and he's charged with the murder of Amanda Davies. The guards took him out of the receiving area, and everyone was huddled by the door, scrambling to get a peek. Ivory Murrow is out in the hallway yelling with his dark-brown skin and glistening shaved head reflecting the light above.

By seven thirty, Deputy Kady came to the door.

"Parker," he called.

"Yes," I replied.

"You won't be going out till noon."

"That's after my interview time, though!"

"I told you that earlier."

Then fifteen minutes later, Kady called me out for the interview. He escorted me to Post One, where Claude Thomas was waiting. That left us little time to prepare.

"They tried to stop us from doing this interview," I said, taking a deep breath.

"Don't worry about that now, Phil. Just let them know how you maintain and tell them that our affinity is the reason for me being your lawyer," he replied, patting me on the back.

I took a few deep breaths, trying to let out the tension on my way to the library. Shelby Wiezek from *Channel 10 News* is waiting to take my statement. He looks a lot thinner than he did on television, and from my view on the other side of the glass, I see an awkward, tall, middle-aged, rather lanky White guy with a military-style crew cut staring back at me. He has gray hair and a thin black mustache. He is wearing a red polo shirt, tan slacks, and slip-on black penny loafers. I anxiously waited for him to turn on his tape recorder.

"You don't mind me taping our conversation, Phil?"

"No, not at all," I replied before setting the phone against my ear.

"Thank you for meeting with me."

"No, thank you."

"Who is that you got with you?" he asked, shifting his attention to Claude.

"Claude Thomas, my lawyer."

"I thought that Stuart Dunnings was handling your case?"

"Claude is representing me in another matter."

"Okay, whatever you say. Tell me about your case."

"Well, this is not just a case about rape, it's a case about race. After my release, Claude Thomas will represent me in my case against Michigan State University for my wrongful termination."

"How so, Phil? How does this rape allegation correlate with racism?"

"It bleeds racism. From the day I was charged until now, I've been moving through a gauntlet of disappointments and degradations. The way MSU, the police, and the judicial system handled these outlandish accusations is nothing short of a witch hunt. From the very beginning, the alleged victim admitted that she never said no and testified as having only one drink with me. I don't see how one drink could have rendered her too intoxicated to have consented in the act of which she was fully aware and took part in."

"You're referring to the sexual act?"

"Yes, I am. Then after I went home, Jane continued drinking and barhopping."

"She testified to this? In court?"

"Yes, she did, right in front of the judge, jury, and everyone else."

"Then what happened, Phil? When did you start to feel like your chances of being exonerated were slipping away?"

"The moment they tried to use my polygraph statement against me. A polygraph statement is supposed to be inadmissible, but the judge allowed it."

"Your lawyer didn't object?"

"He did not."

"What was the conflict in the polygraph statement?"

"During my initial statement, I didn't tell the cops everything."

"What did you withhold?"

"I didn't tell them that Jane and I had sex."

"Why didn't you admit to this?"

"I was embarrassed, and I never expected this thing to become a rape charge."

"So what evidence did the prosecution have to prove that you spiked her drink?"

"None at all. There were no drugs found in Jane's system."

"Was she able to walk out of the bar on her own?"

"Yes. They tried to crucify me based on the statement of two witnesses that only observed her for less a minute."

"Who were these witnesses?"

"Initially, after we left the restaurant, she was complaining that she had to use the bathroom, so I took her to the house owned by one of my close friends since it was the nearest possible restroom to our location. Unfortunately, when I knocked on the door, I was confronted by one of his tenants."

"What was the root of the conflict?"

"Well, he didn't want to let us in, so I took the back way inside the house."

"The back way?"

"Yes, the back door was open, so we let ourselves inside. After Jane finished using the bathroom, they spotted us on our way out."

"Was she having trouble walking?"

"No, she was just quiet. That's just how she was. They completely blew things out of proportion."

"So you're saying that these tenants had something against you?"

"Yes, I think they didn't like seeing a Black man with a White woman."

"Were they White?"

"Yes, they were."

"Did the confrontation escalate the second time they saw you?"

"Yes, it did. We almost came to blows. He got up in my personal space, but I just left."

"Beyond that, what do you think led to your conviction?"

I paused, sliding my fingertips against the stubble across my chin. I thought about the case, about those moments in court, and then it hit me. The realization was just beginning to dawn, that perhaps the problem was my representation.

"I wasn't prepared on the stand, and by the way that I presented, I might have lost the jurors."

"What do you mean by that?"

"I meant the jurors might have thought that I wasn't as credible as the alleged victim."

"Well, you certainly have a story to tell, Phil. Thanks again for talking to me today, but I think that should be enough."

"Thank you," I said, rising to my full height.

Claude was there right by my side, and I felt comfortable with him.

"So how do you think it went, Phil?" he asked.

"I'm happy with the interview. I feel we covered all the major issues."

At twelve thirty, Kady came in to transport me to court. I rode in the back of the police van, handcuffed to several inmates. The driver was a wild man. He's a bit older than the other guards. He looked to be in his late sixties, and he had a gray crew cut hiding underneath his blue baseball cap and a thick, salt-and-pepper gray mustache. I looked out of the window, watching the orange and red tree leaves while they swayed in the breeze. The wind was whispering in my ear. It felt so refreshing to be out in the elements again.

We arrived at the Lansing Police Department about twenty minutes late, and there to greet us was the bailiff. She's middle-aged, tall, blond, and dressed like a lawyer. She was wearing a black dress, red lipstick, and black high-heeled pumps. Eventually, I found myself in a cell with an older Indian man. He's kicking around a roll of toilet paper, and he seemed to be amusing himself.

"So what are you in here for?" I asked, leaning against the cold cement wall.

"Aggravated assault!" he replied while pulling at the white stubble of his beard.

Minutes later, several inmates started milling in.

Finally, an older, dark-skinned Black man approached me, shaking his head. Fred Davis was tall and morbidly obese.

"I could've gotten off," he lamented.

"So what's your name?" I asked.

"Fred. Just call me Fred. So what's your deal?"

"I was charged with criminal sexual assault."

"Oh, date rape, huh?"

"Yeah, I guess."

"My ex put me here. They said I was trespassing on her property."

"Trespassing?"

"I was drunk. I shouldn't have been there."

"Yeah, when a woman's fed up, it's over."

"When it's over, it's over."

"So did you do it? Did you slip something in Jane Snow's drink, Parker?"

"Oh no, of course not, I would never do that.'

"Then why the hell are you here?"

"I was railroaded."

"Yeah, that's what they all say."

"Well, I'm telling you the truth," I replied, looking directly into his quivering brown eyes.

"Well, I hope they place me in Grand Rapids Residential Treatment Center. Any place is better than jail."

"I hear you," I grunted while the guard suddenly opened the cell door.

"Phil Parker," the short, blond guard called out.

"I'm here," I replied, following him to the receiving room where Stuart was awaiting my arrival.

We went into a small, dimly lit room for a briefing. He looked flustered. He was wearing a black suit, a plaid shirt, and a black tie.

"Phil, I'm extremely disappointed in your public statements about the conspiracy issue."

"Whose side are you on?" I asked.

"I have no basis without any evidence."

"I have two witnesses to back up my statements. And one you already knew about."

"Let's just stick to the facts from now on," he replied before leading me to the courthouse.

We took a seat near the jury box as the last few stragglers rushed into the courtroom. The room was packed, and when Brown walked in, you could hear a pin drop. Judge Brown was thin, short, and sallow. He had wavy white hair, a square beardless chin, and blue eyes. He glanced over at me, covering his mouth with his hands.

"I will not support your conspiracy theory," Dunnings whispered under his breath.

"Then just say no comment," I replied, shrugging my shoulders.

When I looked up, I found Judge Brown staring back at me with brooding eyes. Stuart stood up, presented his arguments, and the prosecution followed. The prosecutor, Linda Berryman, concluded her discussion by stating that I had been making statements to the press about a conspiracy. After a few moments of silence, the judge denied the motion, but he said he would take some time to consider the polygraph issue.

"I will make my ruling in two weeks," he announced before hammering his gavel against the smooth wood of the bench.

"What a flippant," I muttered under my breath.

"I don't watch the news. Instead I like to watch mystery movies," Brown casually joked as he stood to his full height, gathering his paperwork.

"I don't watch that station either, plus I have no involvement in a conspiracy issue," Stuart said, approaching the bench with his briefcase in hand.

I was shocked that he openly supported Judge Brown's antagonism. I was questioning my choice of an attorney again and again. It was becoming clear that Stuart Dunnings did not have my best interests in mind.

David Garner, *Channel 10 News*, and Clarence Thomas were amongst the many onlookers in the courtroom, now rising from their seats. They quickly carted us inmates out in handcuffs. We went into the holding area and ate dry spaghetti and garlic bread burnt around the edges.

After dinner, we stripped down and returned to our cells. Jasper was sitting on the side of his bunk when I entered the room.

"We didn't see the news today. How'd it go?" Jasper asked in a low tone.

"I think that my appeal was denied. Why didn't you see the newscast?"

"Man, Deputy Johnson was on. That hard nose didn't even turn on the TV!"

"Wow, what a trip," I replied as Ernie from Dorm *E* walked past the cell, giving me the thumbs up.

Ernie is short, but his body's chiseled. He was the youngest and craziest Mexican inmate in the correctional facility. I went to the phones feeling good about the day. The line went quickly, and before I even knew it, I was calling Judy Becker.

"Hey, Judy. How are you?"

"Good. And, Phil, I watched the interview."

"You watched it?"

"They showed a shot of you saying it's not about rape, it's about race. Also, the *State News* did an extensive article about your case."

"That's good. We need to let the public know what happened back there in court."

"You're right, Phil. They wrongfully convicted you, and it's just not right."

"I'm not saying that I'm a perfect man, but I did not take advantage of that woman."

"We know that. I know that!"

"I appreciate your support. Thank you for being a friend, Judy."

Judy and I said our goodbyes, and when I got back to Dorm *C*, Jasper was shaving. I moved down the hallway and went into my cell to find Elder Bryant waiting for me. He had silver hair, a broad nose, a crooked jaw, and black circles around those dark-brown eyes. We read Psalm 34 and Colossians 3 and then he sat down beside me on my bunk.

"I saw you on television this afternoon. Keep the faith, Phil," Elder Bryant said, looking me in the eyes on his way out.

Ace is thirty-four but looked at least ten years younger. He's handsome, Black, and burly, and he always kept a new taper. I watched him out in the hall, surrounded by a small group of inmates.

"I wrote a poem for y'all. This is a little something that I composed during my first month of incarceration."

Prison is families separated.
Mothers, fathers, sons, and daughters.
It is our road map down the darkest
    depths,
The impulsive actions break the lives of
    those dressed in orange uniforms.
We reside where innocence is torn.
There's no fancy flowing colors, no van-
    ity in the wardrobe of criminals.
We're sentenced with the pack to be
    less, behind these walls,
Holding cuff lines on our wrists along
    walks down penitentiary halls.
And by the stroke of light, I find
    myself again, turning through the
    coldest nights,
The hard blows they give
To those condemned
We live in a place where the sun never
    shines.
Doomed in the home where sentences
    live, and street thugs are martyrs
    at times.
Both the innocent and guilty lie
Paying for their crimes with their lives
I hear them crying in the night while
    some search for daylight.
Still, others wait, sinking more in-depth
    into the darkness

Lions are kings in the den of animals
    and thieves.
Hate brews as killers lick their wounds.
Eyes are dry where compassion is cold
    as icicles dripping out in Michigan
    snow.
The heat burns relentlessly in cages
    where the air is always dry.
There is no hope for those who cannot
    see the sky.
The deeds committed have left us here
    to be judged by hate, rage, and fear.
A day is a year while these walls sweat,
    blood, and tears.
Beasts of the cage seal pacts
Alone to be stalked like prey,
Enduring pain and suffering through
    each perilous day,
Still, we find a way to get through the
    hard time.
Again, I close my eyes while one morn-
    ing becomes a hundred more,
I see pasture springing with wild daf-
    fodils stretching for miles.
Only to awaken to the smell of iron
    bars, choking air.
There's no neutrality in a war to feel
    again,
Freedom is a lost cause where I'm living,
Learning to hate while losing my inno-
    cence in prison.

Ace concluded, taking a bow before the
crowd. Kady's voice distracted my attention from
the group now gathered around Ace.

171

"Phil, you've just received some mail," he said, handing me a manila envelope.

"Thanks," I replied, eagerly finding a spot on the edge of my cot.

Once seated, I ripped open the envelope and retrieved a copy of the *State News*. I eagerly skimmed through the entire paper until I found the article about my case. "Judge Brown Denies Parker's Motion for a New Trial." As I read deeper into the article, it also stated that one of my motions was considered because of the polygraph issue. I am pleased that publicity exposed this motion. I know that there were many apprehensions in the beginning and even more suspicion after our court hearing. I am ready to continue this crusade toward uncovering the truth about what happened that night at the Park Inn. This case was like a puzzle, and the pieces seemed to be now falling into place.

After reading the article, I'm looking through the *USA Today* newspaper when I came across a disturbing report. The death of a Black teenager found hanging in his cell by his shoelaces has caused public outrage. One pathologist theorized that it is theoretically impossible for one to commit suicide in the manner alleged. The poor soul was probably dead hours before the lynching. In Jackson, Mississippi, the incident happened in a jail where forty-two Black inmates have died under mysterious circumstances since 1987.

January 22, 1993

I woke up around lunchtime and gave my breakfast to Ace, and after devouring heaps of plastic-tasting macaroni and cheese and an order of dry, brick-hard meatloaf, I played cards with Jasper and Todd. It was cutthroat through two intense games, but still, I lost both. My money order didn't come today, so I was hoping to win instead of borrow; but there was no luck there. The dorm is calm, and time flew by until Jasper and Todd started going at it again.

"Get your hand out of my pocket!" Jasper yelled, rising to his full height.

"My hand ain't in anybody's pocket," Todd shouted, jumping into Jasper's personal space, and before anyone even knew it, they were standing nose to nose.

"You were looking at my cards," Jasper said, clenching his fists.

"I didn't do any such thing. Don't blame me because you're a sore loser, Jasper!"

"Todd, you ain't shit but a short, square peckerwood!" Jasper replied.

Deputy Sellik quickly got between them, and they were both put on lockdown.

Later that night, I reread the article in the *State News* about my case, and I became highly optimistic about my hopes for a new trial. I think the polygraph issue has created serious questions about Brown's denial. Before I went to sleep, I fell on my knees and asked God to help me through this ordeal.

January 23, 1993

Don and Ace are up early today. Ace is going crazy, threatening to break everything. I think he's trying to create a stir, so he'll be shipped out. The guy needs a cigarette to calm down because if not, the guards' libel to rush in there and beat him down again. I moved into the recreation room, preparing to watch the *NBA All-Star Game*, and Jasper was getting into it with Todd. They were standing chest to chest right in front of the television screen.

"Your breath smells like wolf pussy," Jasper said, pushing Todd back.

The entire room echoed with laughter, causing Todd to turn beet red. He quickly rushed out of the room, saddened because the other inmates found Jasper's insult so hilarious. Sellik is on today, and he's an asshole when it comes to breaking the doors. I'm looking forward to my meeting with Claude later this afternoon. I sent a kite to have Elder Bryant preach here addressed to the jail administrator. A few hours later, Kady came to my room.

"Phil, you've received a message."

"From who?"

"Claude Thomas. He's not gonna be in to see you today due to the weather."

"Oh, is it that bad out there?"

"We had some serious snowfall, about seven inches to be exact, or maybe even more by this time of day."

"Wow, it must be freezing on those Michigan streets."

"You'd probably be better off in here."

"I don't think so," I said, watching him walk away wearing a cynical smile.

Later that night, Jasper was cheating again on the card table, and other inmates noticed. He cheated both games, so I lost my cool.

"You owe me a candy bar because of your damn cheating," I said, looking him up and down. It was payback time, and I was coming to collect my dues.

"Man, pipe down. I don't owe you anything!" Jasper intoned.

"You do, Jas, it is payback time, and I think you know what that means. So don't try to sell me out. Naw, not even for a minute."

"Okay, man! Calm down!"

"I will if you do!"

"Just meet me halfway, man."

"Keep it real, Jasper, just keep it real," I said, pointing toward the mess hall.

I was snickering under my breath while watching him sulk.

CHAPTER 13

Chaos Unfiltered

January 24, 1993

Sellik is working this morning. Franklin, one of the cart attendants, came in to distribute the most recent copy of the *State News*. Franklin Roxy was short in stature, and he had small, tawny eyes. His physique was gaunt; and he kept his face beardless, and his head shaved. I paid out nine items, and then as he was leaving, I read that someone contaminated our chili with urine. One of the trustees, Demetrius Errol, later confessed to the crime. News of this traveled through the block like wildfire, and within an hour, Jasper, Bruce, and I were treading the halls to see Deputy Perez and issue our complaints personally. When we got to his office, Perez leaned against the wall with his hands on his gun belt. Being 5'4" and 145 pounds, Perez is the classic example of an angry little man with something to prove.

"I wanna see Lt. Vissar," I demanded, folding my arms across my chest.

"What's this all about?" Perez replied.

"It's about the piss in our chili on Saturday!" Bruce chimed in.

"He's busy right now. I'll pass the message!" Perez barked.

"We're all in an uproar about it, and we don't like it one bit," I said.

"Hey, at this point, it's just a rumor. So don't be alarmed. We will keep you updated on the progress of our investigation," Perez explained.

"Two people told me that it happened, but they didn't see it," I said in a low tone.

"I want names," Perez grunted, looking into my eyes.

"I'm not giving up any names," I responded, shaking my head.

"I understand that you don't want to rat on anyone," Perez muttered before pulling me aside from the group.

"We're just concerned about our health with the AIDS epidemic and all!" I intoned.

"I understand. We'll continue our investigation tomorrow," Perez said before turning his back and walking away from us.

"Can you believe it, Phil?" Jasper inquired, leading us down the quiet aisles.

"And if Dorm *C* caught wind of this, they might riot," Bruce said, energetically rubbing his right shoulder.

"You all right, man?" I asked.

"Yeah, I probably pulled something while playing basketball yesterday," Bruce admitted, cringing.

January 25, 1993

After exercising, I tried to call Stuart, but he wasn't in. Moments later, his secretary informed me that he'd be back around two thirty. Since last Wednesday, I haven't heard from him, and with each passing day, I lose more confidence in him. When I arrived back in my room, Elder Bryant is at the door. We were going over Ephesians 4 when Sellik came to the door looking flushed.

"Phil, Claude Thomas is here to see you," he said, tapping his baton against the wall.

I thanked Elder Bryant before following Sellik's lead to the visitation area. Claude was there, dressed casually in a red polo, navy-blue slacks, and black dress shoes.

"What happened the other day?"

"The other day?"

"When you missed our appointment."

"Oh, sorry about that, Phil. I was busy. I saw Stuart in Gazy's court the other day."

"Did he say anything to you?"

"Not a word. All Stuart does is move through the motions. I can assist you in finding someone else to represent you for the appeal. One of my lawyer friends looked at your MSU material and discovered how petty Kathy is. It is obvious that she had a personal vendetta against you."

"Thank you, Claude. I will consider that option, but right now, I think we're in way too deep to turn back now."

"Okay, Phil, just keep me posted."

"Later," I muttered, watching him walk away.

After talking to Claude, I went back to my room to read the most recent letter from Peggy,

Landon, and Ann. Landon transferred to a different school, and he likes it. Ann is doing great, and Peggy's hanging in there like a champ. I held her letter against my chest for a while, slipping in and out of consciousness. Tonight, I dreamt of being back with my family; oh, how I miss them so.

January 26, 1993

The day began with Deputy Sellik having a snit fit over a stolen plastic bag. The guards went from cell to cell, looking for a culprit. About twenty minutes later, they brought Bouee out in handcuffs. His dreadlocks were whipping wildly down his back while they marched him to lockdown. He was still allowed to take a shower and go to the twelve-thirty workshop, but I bet he'll think twice before stealing any garbage bags. Bryan Faust was on at 8:00 a.m. Recreation was fun. Gordon ended up being captain, and he made sure to choose the team with Jasper, Freddy, and Newman on it. All of them are tall, Black, and excellent basketball players. We played competitively, but our team ended up losing both games by a small margin. I wrote a kite to Major Carpenter concerning the mail tampering and corruption that's been going on. I missed too many letters and pictures from Peggy. These are the small freedoms that keep us going, and to deny me that would be the purest form of cruel and unusual punishment. I won't ever let them take away my hope. As I wrote a letter to Peggy, an older African American man with processed hair and crooked teeth was peering through the door.

"You Phil?" he asked.

"Yeah, who the hell wants to know?" I replied, rising to my full height.

"Jay does. I just wanted to pass a message."

"What?"

"Don't forget about the papers," he grunted before continuing on his way.

He's a dark-skinned brother in a black tank top and orange uniform pants. I guess if you start something in here, it eventuates into expectations. It is gym day, and I was looking forward to a good cardio workout after breakfast. While blowing my nose at the table, I noticed Gordon giving me a dirty look. Gordon's a burly, middle-aged, light-skinned ex-marine with a shaved head and broad shoulders. I recall the time he and Bruce got into it because he felt Bruce wasn't mannerly. Ben, Bruce, and Jasper were present, and Gordon was at the far end of the table with his dark-brown eyes fixated on me now.

"Anybody who doesn't like anything that I do, here's the aisle, come get it," I said, looking at Gordon the whole time.

Deputy Sellik tapped me on the shoulder from behind. "Phil, Major Carpenter, wants to speak with you," he muttered as he watched the crowd of inmates while holding his gun belt.

I stood up and followed him down the hall to his office.

"Phil, have a seat," Carpenter said, from a seated position behind his desk.

I took a seat in one of the vacant chairs by the door.

Carpenter's a short man with a faint, white mustache and a round belly. There's a horde of freckles specked around his brow, and he was balding around the crown of his head.

"I received your kite," he calmly said in a quiet tone.

"I'm about fed up with the conditions here," I replied.

"There's no conspiracy or tampering with your mail. I just wanted to make my point clear. Now, I'm aware there should be better uniformity when dealing with your mail because this incident is said to have happened on several occasions."

"I wanna know when is the harassment going to stop?"

"The procedural manual is outdated, but I assure you it's currently being revised." ·

"Well, several items, including letters and pictures of mine, have been sent back. I don't see how any of these items violated policy as stated in the current handbook."

"Well, honestly, Phil, I'm not completely aware of everything that happens around here, but I'll look into it."

"I've seen other inmates receiving books and shoeboxes full of pictures, and I don't see why I'm denied those freedoms. My sister Terry sent me a book last month, and it was returned."

"What was the title?"

"*Black Rage, White Justice.*"

"Well, I can see why they sent it back."

"They called it contraband, but it was just a book, and this was unjust."

"Give us some time to ascertain the whereabouts of your letters, and we'll get to the bottom of this."

"I wanted to bring this to your attention so that you are aware of what's going on."

"Well, Phil, before I forget, I wanted to inform you that your wife, Peggy, will be here to visit you soon. You have to arrange a special visit. You are eligible to schedule the visit between the hours of eight to five. I think we've gone out of our way to treat you a little better than the other inmates."

"How is that?"

"By allowing you media visits."

"I have the right to speak with the media. The policy clearly states that if I've been sentenced and have no charges pending, then the media can come in. So don't think for one second that I'm getting preferential treatment."

"We'll keep in touch, these things take time."

"Yeah, I know all about time," I replied, heading for the door.

Later that evening, I found myself in a cut-throat card game with Todd, Moss, and Jasper. Todd stood up and threw his cards on the table. He was set at a five bid.

"What the fuck is that?" Todd growled. "Do you have a problem with me, Coach?" he yelled while surging toward me.

"You can come to my room, or I'll go to yours. If you wanna wrestle, then we can go anytime, chump," I said, shooting to my feet.

"I can outbox you. We can do this right here in the foyer."

"No, we can't do it right here because then, Deputy Perez would be able to save you. I don't want to leave you with an escape route," I replied, squaring my feet while Todd walked away.

Hours later, I was thinking of a title for this stage of trials and tribulations in my life. Jasper was lying on the bottom bunk, dozing off.

"Jas, you awake?" I quietly asked.

"Yeah, Phil."

"I was thinking of a title for the fall of the MSU wrestling coach Phil Parker."

"What is it, Phil?"

"White Web."

"Why that title?"

"I see myself as an insect that has encountered a web of injustice for my tryst with a White woman."

January 27, 1993

Deputy Perez is on today, and the whole dorm was watching Sally Jesse Rafael. The theme of this episode was a discussion about police rape. One young White lawyer was talking about how false accusations destroy people's lives. Now everything was beginning to make sense to me as I sat there, trying to piece together the puzzle. How did I end up here? It seemed as if I was just a breath away from my former life as a successful head wrestling coach. It was hard to believe that my journey that began back in North Chicago was over. I felt I had so much more still to offer the wrestling world. It was hard knowing in my heart what happened in that car, knowing that Jane and I had consensual sex, knowing that she wasn't drunk, knowing that she did not indicate that she didn't want me to go as far as we did. If I could go back, I would, if only I would've seen her true intentions when she initially approached me.

January 29, 1993

We had chili for dinner today, and we all took it as a slap in the face. Dorm *B* threw their portions on the trustee, and Sellik had to come down to break up the crowd. I smelled my tray before eating. Meals were few and far between in the Ingham County Jail. Bill was the only one from my dorm who didn't eat. I skipped my exercise routine to attend an early church service. Paul Garret was the acting preacher, and today we read from Romans 10, 35, and 39. Paul is a small and quiet little Irishman with blond hair and blue eyes. When he looked at us, he was colorblind. He saw us only as human beings and followers of God. After church, I went into my room and wrote until the lights went off.

March 1, 1993

It is the first day of a new month, and I am nearing the end of my incarceration. I exercised this morning and found myself imagining the taste of the wind on my lips when the day comes to walk out of jail and into my new life. Deputy Sellik is on, and his mood is one of intolerance. Word on the block is that a cult in Waco killed four agents and seventeen others in a shootout. Their leader, David Koresh, doesn't look to be backing down an inch. Don and Bruce are sulking because they didn't ride out today. Dorm *C* was quiet until about 2:00 p.m. while Big Ben watched *Donahue*, and Todd and Don's card game broke the peace. Ben is 6'5", 285 pounds, light-skinned, and African American. This former Golden Gloves champion is rugged from head to toe, and everyone knew not to mess with him. He kept his hair coarse and wild, and he had thick eyebrows, a thin nose, and high cheekbones. Ben huffed and puffed for a while before finally deciding to jump up and vent his rage.

"Y'all need to quiet the fuck down. Can't you see that I'm trying to watch television here?" Ben is bellowing while stretching his arms out in a threatening manner.

"Fuck you, Ben. I can do what I want to do!" Todd replied, and at that moment, Ben just went ballistic.

He charged toward Todd with his fists clenched, and when he got close enough, he didn't hesitate to swing. Todd ducked the first jab, but Ben followed up with a left hook. One hit is all it took to end this confrontation. It took at least twenty seconds for Todd to regain consciousness. Don didn't speak about the incident until Ben had left the room.

"You'd better watch yourself, Ben!" He yelled while helping Todd to his feet.

Later, things cooled off, and the block was peaceful and quiet. I made my way to the phones looking to call Natalie Barna.

"Hey, Phil," she said in a low tone.

"How's it going, Natalie?"

"You tell me."

"Did you hear anything about the appeal?"

"Judge Brown hasn't fully delivered a decision on all motions as of yet."

"Okay, keep me posted."

"I will."

"And Natalie, please don't give up on me."

"Hang in there, Phil."

"Talk to you later," I said, setting the phone back on the receiver.

When I got back to my cell, the captain called me out. Captain Jess Smith stood only 5'7" but was a meaty hulk of a man. He is one of the few fifty-two-year-olds still capable of holding their own with the younger inmates. Smith keeps his white hair freshly spiked, and he was always clean-shaven.

"Phil, *Channel 6* wants to interview you tomorrow. Maybe you're getting too many visits from the press," Captain Smith said.

"Anytime the press wants to come in here and interview, I have no complaints. And any time they call, I wish to be notified," I replied.

Fortunately, the captain's attempt to unnerve me worked in reverse. I immediately left my cell and went back to the phones to call Claude Thomas.

"Hey, Phil. What's up?"

"I'm being interviewed by *Channel 6 News* tomorrow, and I wanted to know if you wanted to be in on it?"

"Yes, I will be there."

"Please bring the three letters I gave you."

"Three letters?"

"Yes, the letters from Carl Adams, Bobby Douglas, and Harold Nichols."

"I will bring the whole file."

"Great."

"And I've contacted the Civil Rights Department hoping to set up a meeting."

"What was their response?"

"I haven't heard anything yet. I will send a registered letter to make sure that they receive my request."

"Let's keep the fight going."

"I will be in to see you at 9:30 a.m. tomorrow."

"See you then, Claude," I said, hanging up the phone.

Later on that evening, Jas, Gordon, and I were playing spades. Jasper ended up getting himself set for the second time.

"Get down, Jasper, and do your push-ups," I said, pointing to the floor.

"Maybe I should disclose what you said about Paul last night," Jasper loudly replied.

Paul was standing in the lobby shuffling his feet. I was shocked that Jasper would betray my confidentiality right in front of everyone.

"Why don't you tell Paul what you think of him?" Jasper said with Paul nearing our table.

"You're a snake," I muttered, shaking my head.

"Tell him that you think he's a low-down, dirty Uncle Tom."

Paul stopped dead in his tracks and then looked up at me with these sad, puppy-dog eyes.

"I thought we were friends," he moaned before continuing on his way.

Paul was one of the only inmates in Block *C* within my age group. We were considered leaders of the Black community in the dorm. On the outside, he looked like your average overweight, balding, brown-skinned brother, but behind these walls, Paul was a prime target. He didn't belong here, and everyone knew it. He's doing time for spousal abuse, but we all knew that he got a bum rap. His old lady wanted to get him back after catching him in bed with a younger woman. I couldn't believe that Jasper would betray my confidence. I got up and went to my cell, looking to absorb my thoughts and energy into preparing for my interview tomorrow. I don't need any additional distractions. Drey suddenly burst into my cell, pounding his chest with his fist.

"What do you want?" I asked, rising to my full height.

"It's my last night, and I just wanted to let you know how good it's going to be not to have to smell the stench of your stinking feet anymore."

"Yeah, I'm excited about the fact that I don't have to see your ugly face around here another day."

"What happened to you, Phil?"

"Who are you to talk with your jailhouse manners and dirty cornrows?"

"I'm Drey, the Night Creeper, and don't you forget it!"

"Well, I'm Coach Parker, and don't you forget that!"

I watched him walk down the aisle and then I took a seat on my bunk. I was racking my brain with thoughts while mentally preparing for tomorrow's interview as Jasper came into the room.

"Hey, Phil, I just got back from my Alcoholics Anonymous meeting. You wouldn't believe who I spoke to."

"I don't even want to hear it. How could you stab me in the back like that?"

"Oh, you're trying to call me a backstabber?"

"If it walks like a dog, and it looks like a dog, then it's a dog."

"I spoke to Paul. So don't worry—I smoothed things out."

"I can't trust anyone in here."

"Well, maybe you can't. I just wanted to let you know that I didn't mean to disrespect you, Coach."

"Yeah, I don't care because the damage is already done."

"I believe you."

"What?"

"I believe you. I know that the girl lied on you."

"You don't betray someone and then apologize."

"Well, good luck with your interview."

I grunted while turning away. I could hear Jasper cursing under his breath as I closed my eyes and fell fast asleep.

March 2, 1993

I got up at 7:30 a.m. and exercised in my cell. Jasper was lying on his bunk, feeling guilty. I noticed that he didn't bring my laundry in from the lounge area.

"Man, I'm tired of these Hunkies in here. Did you know that Chris and Ben are in here for messing with kids?" he said in a low tone.

A good night's rest was enough to quell my anger, and as far as I was concerned, Jasper was the least of my problems.

"Wow, I had no clue."

"I'm not going to have anything to do with anyone anymore."

"Just do you."

"Yeah, whatever you say, Coach."

"You're the one who can't keep their mouth shut."

"Are you calling me a snitch?" he snarled while angrily approaching me with his fist clenched.

"Back your ass up before I have to put you down," I warned, pushing him back.

"Man, we used to be cool."

"I thought that you were trustworthy."

"Whatever, man."

"Yeah, whatever," I replied before walking out into the aisles.

I heard footsteps trailing me, and I turned around to face Deputy Sellik.

"I wanted to inform you that *Channel 6 News* has canceled your interview today. You should give them a call," he said, and I noticed a trace of sympathy in his tone.

"I will," I replied before making my way to the phones.

I was trying my best not to fall into depression, but I felt the weight of the world on my shoulders. It wasn't about saving my career anymore; it was about proving the truth. So I picked up the phone and dialed one of my media contacts, Maria Garcia.

"Hello," her soft, sultry voice was soothing to my ears.

I knew at that moment that I had to make a connection.

"Hey, Maria. I just heard that you wouldn't be coming today for our interview."

"I just don't have the time to do it before I leave the country. So let's reschedule for some time in the first week of April."

"Yes, I want to do it. I think it's time to tell my side of the story."

"Yes, it's important that both sides of the story are told."

"There was a deputy that came to me and validated the possibility of a conspiracy."

"He should come forward."

"It might be hard to convince him to put it all on the line. The guy needs to look out for himself."

"They could protect his identity."

"I will try, but the tough part is connecting with him again."

"Well, we'll talk more when I come back from my trip."

"A'right, talk to you then," I said before hanging up the phone.

I felt saddened by the delay. After talking to Maria, I decided to call Natalie Barna to update on the status of my case.

"Phil, how are you?"

"I'm hanging in there. How are you, Natalie?"

"Good, just a little busy."

"Have you heard anything?"

"The judge denied the motion for a new trial in your case."

"That's a tough pill to swallow."

"Keep your head up, Phil."

"I will."

"Well, take care, Phil."

"Later," I mumbled.

I was numb after hearing the news. Why was Stuart acting so callous these days?

I came to a decision right then and there to part ways with Stuart Dunnings. Claude Thomas met me in the visitation area two hours later, dressed in a black suit, a black dress shirt, black pants, and black penny loafers. He's clean cut, bright eyed, and filled with positive energy.

"How are you holding up, Phil?'

"I'm all right."

"So I take it that you heard the verdict."

"I heard about it on the news."

"Stuart did not attempt to contact you about it?"

"He did not."

"That's a red flag. I'm beginning to wonder if Stuart was ever really in your corner."

"Maybe my choice of a lawyer was a big mistake."

"Well, I will be aggressive with the Civil Rights Department. If we have them on our side, we're sure to make some waves. Let's keep the faith, my brother," he said, half-smiling at me behind the glass.

I was glad to have him working for me. We locked eyes, and for a moment, I saw a glimpse of myself in him. It was like looking into a mirror at the man that I used to be on the outside. I thought back to when I was a million miles away from these cold steel bars. Now I find myself trapped behind these pale jailhouse walls. When I arrived back at the dorm, I noticed Jasper hawking me in an attempt to regain my trust. He followed me to the recreation area.

Recreation was fun today. Jasper and I played against Gordy and Chris in three games of two-on-two. Gordy was second in command for the Blacks. Word in the dorm is that he was once a high-ranking Vice Lord, but he left the gang five years ago in light of his brother's murder. Gordy was broad-shouldered, muscular, and tall. He always kept his hair tied in tight cornrow braids. Tommy Gordy rarely smiled, but he was primarily an honorable individual. Even here, there was honor amongst thieves.

Chris threw Gordy the ball about mid court, where the young man decided to try and take it to the hole. While Gordy dribbled to the hoop, I reached out for the ball, and he twisted his ankle and went tumbling to the floor. We watched him swaying from side to side for a few awkward seconds.

"Okay, Parker, don't you do that again," he grunted, rising to full height.

"Just play the game. I barely touched you. Don't blame me because you lost your balance," I said, folding my arms over my chest.

"You undercut me," he shot back.

"If you can't take the heat, then just get out of the kitchen," I replied, squaring my feet.

And before he even knew it, I had taken the ball from his trembling hands. I took a shot from the three-point line, and the ball went right into the rim.

"Nice shot, Coach," Jasper said, raising his right fist in the air.

"We won, so y'all know what that means," I muttered, leading us off the basketball court.

"Two cakes each," Jasper said, chuckling under his breath.

Chris and Gordy went in separate directions. I could see this loss hurt their pride. When I returned to my cell, Lt. Vissar and Deputy Sellik were quarreling with Shannon. They were bringing him in from maximum security to Dorm *C*.

"Fuck y'all peckerwoods. Get your filthy hands off me!" Shannon's voice rose above the din while he desperately tried to break free.

Fifteen minutes later, they called in the Goon Squad to drag him back to maximum security. I then made my way to the phones, looking to call home. The line dwindled quickly, and before I knew it, I was holding the phone against my ear, hoping to hear my mother's voice.

"Hey, Phil," Dad's voice was comforting.

"Hey, Dad. How are you doing?"

"I can still kill a bear."

"Hold on, Pop. Don't you go killing any bears. How are you recovering from surgery?"

"I'm fine. There's a little soreness, but overall I'm feeling just fine."

"That's great. I'm glad to hear that."

"Well, son, Momma wanted to say something to you."

"Okay, it was good talking to you, Dad."

"You too, Phil."

After a few moments of silence, Momma came to the phone.

"Phil, I was reading Paul and Silas in the Bible, and I thought of you."

"Really, Mother?"

"The jail opened for them, and they weren't there in the morning. That's what you need to remember. One morning, this nightmare will be over."

"You're right. There's a light at the end of the tunnel. I just hope that I make it out of here in one piece."

"Sometimes, I get teary-eyed when I think about what they did to you."

"Momma, don't worry, my lawyers are working on the appeal."

"I heard that the judge rejected your appeal."

"Yeah, I'm not surprised. We won't give up there."

"Put your trust in God. He won't ever let you down. I'm convinced that the judge won't be too comfortable with his decision. I want to be there when they release you."

"I would love to see you when I walk out of here."

"You hang in there, Phil."

"I will, Mom."

After talking to Mom and Dad, I called Peggy.

"Hey, Phil," she said, answering the call on the first ring.

"Hey, Peg."

"It's so good to hear your voice. I'm thrilled about our visit."

"I'm counting down the minutes, babe."

"Can you believe it, Phil?"

"What?"

"Can you believe that we have to make an appointment just to see each other?"

"It's unbelievable."

"How did we get here, Phil?"

"I should have stayed home that night."

"I know. What you did was morally wrong. Not criminally wrong. We both know that the girl lied."

"She never claimed to have been raped, and that's where the justice system failed us."

"There's no evidence to back up her claim that she passed out in the car. If she passed out in the car, then why did she go on a drinking binge right after the fact?"

"I know, Peg. We know. And one day, the world will know that I didn't rape anyone, in any way, shape, or form."

"You would never do that. It's just not you."

"Be strong, Peg. We will beat this. We know that it wouldn't be easy when we tied the knot, and we did it anyway. Love is our driving force, and love is our motivation. Nothing can ever break our bond. Nothing will ever come between us."

"I love you, Phil. They returned the pictures that I sent you."

"I knew it. I just recently spoke to Major Carpenter about this issue."

"Phil, I promised to take the kids to rent some movies tonight, so I have to get going."

"I love you, Peg."

"I love you too, and don't you ever forget that."

After I hung up the phone, I found myself strolling down the aisles battling the depression and anxiety that weighed down my feet with every step forward. The guards watched, mocking me under their breath. These cold prison walls weren't closing in on me anymore. Now there is a glimmer of hope; now, I had a plan. When I got back to the dorm, I played two hands of spades with Kent and lost them both. I played cutthroat, but regardless, I will be giving up four cakes tomorrow. Kent, Scotch Irish by birth, had a bowl cut, brownish-blond hair, and baby-blue eyes.

March 3, 1993

Deputy Lyons is on today. Lyons is tall, White, blond, and ten years over the hill. He's the most arrogant of all the Caucasian guards.

Jasper stayed in because of a bad cold, and Lyons called his cell check every hour on the half hour. Everyone is on edge around him except me. I refuse to walk on eggshells for any of these fools. I brushed past his shoulder on my way to the phones. I could hear him huffing and puffing behind me.

"Watch where you're going, Parker!" Lyons barked.

I chuckled under my breath, and that only made him look angrier. He was fuming while I picked up the phone and called Judy.

"Phil, I'm glad you called."

"Hey, Judy."

"How are you?"

"I'm fine."

"Pam, the director of the new MSU talk show, is looking forward to hearing from you. Give her a call tomorrow to set something up."

"I will."

"You need to tell your story. Don't let them sweep you under the rug."

"I won't. Believe me, I won't."

"Agitate, Phil."

"We're working on a lawsuit against Michigan State."

"I knew that Brown wouldn't see things your way. The appeal should have been held outside of the Lansing area."

"You're right."

"Your lawyer really let you down on this one."

"That he did."

"I've heard things about him, Phil."

"What have you heard?"

"He's in line for a job with MSU."

"Where did you get this info?"

"Let's just say that I have friends in high places."

"Who would have ever thought in a million years that Stuart was that dirty?"

"Be careful, Phil."

"I will."

"Good talking to you."

"It's always a pleasure to talk to you, Judy," I said before laying the phone on the receiver.

I was feeling slightly dizzy. Was there any truth to what she was telling me about Stuart? And if so, could that be grounds for a new trial? I thought about his comments to the judge during my hearing. He was so quick to make light of my conspiracy theory. I was beginning to see hope, and hope would be my redemption guide. Later that night, I played three games of spades with Todd. It was survival of the fittest. I lost one and won two. After collecting my winnings, I wrote until they shut the lights out.

March 4, 1993

Okin is on today, the same guard that was watching me in my cell a few months ago while I slept. He is a small, awkward country boy. There are rumors that Okin was a skinhead. I picked up my store order and decided to confront him.

"I saw you in my room that morning," I casually said, looking right into his piercing blue eyes.

He just shrugged his shoulders. The smirk on his face told the story of a scared fussy little man. I wanted to grab him by the collar but remained composed. In here, rage can be your best friend, or it can be your worst enemy. As I was walking through Dorm *C*, the commotion was erupting in the aisles. Drew and Bill were engaged in a shouting match. Drew was towering over the much smaller man. Bill was only 5'8", and he had this ridiculously bushy, brown mullet. He would be no match for Drew in a physical confrontation. Bill was the quietest White inmate I had ever met. He barely said more than two words at a time.

Drew, by contrast, is 6'3", Black, and always ready to fight. Drew was raised in the projects of Detroit and is as hard as they come. At twenty-four, he was already a high-ranking Gangster Disciple. He liked to keep his Afro knotty and wild.

"Don't worry about what's under my bed!" Bill exclaimed with his voice cracking under the sound of shuffling feet.

Soon, the two were standing nose to nose, and neither one was showing signs of backing down.

"I'm not your kid. Don't you raise your voice to me," Drew shot back, clenching his fists.

Gordy suddenly stepped between them.

"Whoa. That's my roommate. He just talks loud. Don't take things so personally, Drew," Gordy said, pushing both men back.

"That peckerwood better watch his back," Drew warned, staring into Bill's bloodshot eyes.

"Just play it cool, man," Gordy grunted while leading Bill away from the commotion.

CHAPTER 14

Longing for Freedom

March 5, 1993

Jasper is pacing the room with his shirt off.

"What's the deal with you?" I asked while lying on my bunk, folding my arms over my head. I could feel drops of sweat snaking down my brow.

"I'm worried about my wife. I haven't been able to get a hold of her all week, Phil."

"Don't jump to conclusions."

"She'd better not be fooling around on me," he replied, pounding his fist against the wall.

After our conversation, Jasper shut himself off the rest of the world for a while. I exercised like a madman today, and the whole time I was thinking of my family.

I was thinking about my accomplishments on the wrestling mat. I left behind the type of legacy that should be immutable by the wrestling community. Drew was watching me lift weights, smiling and shaking his head. Chris must have sensed friction in the air and decided to call Drew out on it.

"I'd bet fifty cakes that Coach could handle you," Chris said while reaching out and touching Drew's left shoulder.

Drew was cringing. The look on his face told a thousand words. I could tell that this place was starting to get to Drew. For the past couple of days, I've been experiencing a runny nose, sneezing, and hot flashes and wasn't really in the mood for unnecessary confrontations.

There was an awkward silence between Jasper and me later that evening. The drama only intensified in the television room an hour later. Drew is trying to start some friction by changing the channels back and forth. I decided just to get up and make a call to Pam rather than to engage. I made my way to the phones, preparing myself to make a case to her on how important it is to let me appear on her show. Despite everything they took away from me, I won't ever let them take my pride. I picked up the phone and dialed the number Judy had given me.

"Hello."

"Hello, Pam. It's Phil Parker. I wanted to talk about appearing on your show."

"Phil, I was expecting your call."

"I want to talk about my case."

"Your case intrigues me, especially this racism issue that you have publicly brought up time and time again."

"My case wasn't about rape, it was about race."

"What do you mean by that?"

"What I meant is that there was a collaborated effort by the MSU administration, the prosecution, the police, and the judge to destroy me."

"Do you think there are any other factors involved in the outcome of your case?"

"Oh, yes, I do. Maybe they were just pawns in the plot. Maybe the ring leaders are still out there, hiding in the shadows."

"Who are the ring leaders?"

"Grady Peninger, the former MSU wrestling coach."

"Is he somehow connected with the alleged victim?"

"I feel that someone hired Jane Snow to seduce me and then make this false claim against me."

"You feel Grady hired her."

"Grady rented property to one of her brothers, and her brother was the one that went with her to the police station the night she made her claim."

"Interesting."

"Her false accusations brought me into the judicial system and then the judicial system failed me. I just want my fair day in court. I just want justice. Her lies outweighed the truth, but I know one day, the truth will exonerate me."

"Well, I will get back to you about this, Phil," she said.

"Thanks. Talk to you later, Pam."

March 6, 1993

Today is Timmy's last day. He told me yesterday that he wanted to take sleeping pills after recreation and just pass out. Drew was blasting the radio this morning, and I was fighting the urge just to knock him out cold. Deputy Joe Ryan is on. This Scottish-born immigrant had a fiery temper and an awkward gait. After gym time, we watched *Donahue*, and suddenly, Drew comes bursting into the room shirtless, and unkempt.

"Turn down the fucking television. I'm trying to get some rest here!" he was yelling at the top of his lungs while tying a red bandana over his head.

"You need to calm down!" I replied, waving him off.

His countenance suddenly twisted into a menacing scowl as he surged toward the TV, ripping the plug out of the wall.

"Fuck you, Coach!" he shouted, snarling under his breath.

"No, fuck you, Drew!" I replied, clenching my fists and squaring my feet.

I imagined what I would do to him if he were to cross the line I had drawn for him a long time ago. Then surprisingly, he decided to put the plug back into the socket.

"Just turn it down," he muttered, looking defeated on his way back to his cell.

I was proud of myself for letting him know that I would not be intimidated. Later that evening, Drew marched into the television room, arguing about whether or not we'd watch the news or something else. This time, Jasper had the remote, and he wasn't planning on budging an inch. At this point, most of us were wary of Drew's bullying tactics, and he must have sensed it. He lunged toward Jasper and wrestled away the remote, and that's when Ace stepped in.

"Just let them watch the news. Share the television, Drew," Ace said before stepping into Drew's personal space. "Tensions are high right now, and I don't want to see anyone getting stabbed over what we watch. It's not worth it, man," Ace was pleading with Drew now.

Minutes later, Drew succumbed to the pressure. He stormed out of the room, leaving us to watch whatever most of us wanted to. From then on out, the majority ruled the television. Here was proof that there was still honor amongst the convicted. Later that night, I could hear cursing and screaming coming from Dorm *C*. I was shivering throughout the night. This place is beginning to break me down. Oh, how I wished that I could go back in time and do it all differently. How did I fall into their trap? How did I fall into the white web of militia justice?

I thought of the "Promised Land" that Dr. Martin Luther King referred to in his famous speech about his dream, and it was then that my hope of humankind was restored. I realized that there was still hope for my case, my family, and our nation. So I vowed right then and there that I would survive this ordeal.

March 7, 1993

Timmy was released today, and I've never seen a man look so happy. He was glowing on his last walk through the yard. Deputy Rice is on today. She is one of the few Black female guards in this facility. Though only standing 5'2", Rice was a firecracker of a woman. She wore her dark hair in tight French braids. Today she was particularly tough on everyone. Yet even without makeup, she had well-defined features. Her high cheekbones and cute button nose made her look radiant even when she was frowning. I could hear her voice booming down the aisles.

"Don't you ever call me Dep. You will address me as Deputy!" she intoned very abrasively.

I chuckled under my breath. I was delighted about receiving my doughnut sticks from a store order. Drew is gallivanting around and looking quite pleased because this is his last day. I was shocked when I saw him quietly reading the *Detroit News*. I found myself dragging my feet on my way to my cell. My body was tired and weary, and I couldn't wait to lie down.

March 8, 1993

Peggy just arrived in East Lansing today. She'll be staying with Judy. I couldn't wait to call her. I eagerly made my way to the phones, whistling all the while.

"Hey, Peg."

"Hey, Phil, I am more than ready to talk to Maria Garcia about your canceled interview."

"Take care of business first."

"I am here for you, Phil."

"That's Peg. Fresh off the plane, and you're putting my business first."

"I love you, Phil, and don't you ever forget that."

"I love you too. You taught me to love. You taught me that love is forever. Our bond is eternal. Nothing will ever come between us."

"I can't wait to see you."

"It feels like a dream to be able to be with you again. I spent many sleepless nights thinking about this moment."

"Hang in there, Phil."

"See you soon, Peg," I replied, setting the phone back on the receiver.

It felt so good to hear Peg's sweet voice. She gave me strength, reminding me of who I was. Jasper stopped me in the hall on my way back to Dorm *C*.

"You know good and well that *G* fell on his own accord. You didn't foul him. Can you believe the gall of that chump?" Jas muttered, leaning against the wall.

"I'm not worried about it," I replied, moving past him.

It felt as if his goal was to aggravate the situation. I held back my emotions because at this point, I was trying to leave all the drama behind.

"He's a dirty player," Jasper said, watching me walk away.

I didn't even look back on my way down the aisles. My ultimate goal was to make it out of here in one piece, and to engage myself in a petty conflict would only threaten to defeat my purpose. And just as I turned the corner, I happened to run into Paul.

"How are you doing, Coach?" he asked with a wink.

"I'm just fine."

"I heard that they denied your appeal."

"It's all right. I'm not going to quit fighting for a fair trial. Although, to be honest, I'm not even surprised."

"Don't ever stop fighting," he said, reaching out.

I took his hand, and just like that, our conflict resolved. He leaned over, cupping his hand over his lips.

"Rumors are going around that Jasper is bisexual," he muttered under his breath.

"Wow, you never know these days. Well, you're a stand-up guy in my book," I said while stumbling to my bunk.

And just as my head hit the pillow, Deputy Sellik was at the door.

"Your special visit's here," he said, breaking the door.

I followed his lead, not knowing if it was Peggy or Pam Ozybych here to interview me. It wasn't until we passed the visitation area that I realized Pam was here. She's setting up her lights as I walk into the library. Deputy Sellik and Captain Conatti are in the control area and looking on. Pam was taller than I imagined, her long blond hair was tied in a bun, and she was chewing a stick of bubblegum. She's dressed in a red blazer and black slacks, and her red lipstick was glistening under the overhead lights. Those almond-shaped hazel eyes of hers were hypnotizing.

"Thank you for coming to see me today," I said, taking a seat in front of the camera. "MSU convicted me the minute they found out about charges. They convicted me before I had a chance to defend myself."

"So you feel that they should have supported you early on?"

"As far as they were concerned, I never had a chance. I have retained a lawyer in my lawsuit against the university."

"So you're looking to pursue legal action against the MSU?"

"The success of my lawsuit is contingent on me proving my innocence in a court of law."

"Let's talk evidence. Other than the testimony of the alleged victim, what other evidence did the prosecution present against you?"

"They only had the testimony of two supposed witnesses."

"Who were these witnesses?"

"They were students renting a property from one of my close friends. The male resident is the only one I remember encountering that night. When we got to the door, I introduced myself as a friend of the landlord. I politely asked if Jane could come in to use the bathroom. The young man blatantly refused to let us in. And he got pretty belligerent about it, so we decided just to leave. I checked the back door on our way out, and it was open, so I let myself in. Jane used the bathroom, and on our way out the door, he confronted us. He was fuming about me being in the house, and the situation escalated."

"Was there a fight?"

"We almost came to blows, but I decided to leave before the situation got out of hand. But unfortunately, the guy had it in for me. I think he was still hot over the confrontation when he testified against me for the prosecution."

"So you think he was out to get you?"

"I believe so."

"Was Jane walking straight?"

"She was walking just fine."

"Phil, other than his testimony, was there any other hard evidence presented against you?"

"There was no other evidence presented. So it was just Jane's word against mine."

By this time, Captain Conatti was huffing and puffing in the background. I could see him pacing the room. Gil Conatti is not your average short Italian guy. He kept his salt-and-pepper, gray hair cut low, and talked with a Southern drawl. He had these beady brown eyes, a weak jaw, and yellow teeth.

"You've got ten minutes left," he whispered just loud enough for us all to hear him.

I glanced over my shoulder at him. He shot back a threatening gaze while pacing under the faint light above.

"Don't let them rush you, Pam. Don't feel threatened," I whispered under my breath.

"Well, I want to be courteous."

"I forgot to bring the three letters from Carl Adams, Harold Nichols, and Bobby Douglas. These letters are a testament to my character. I will send them to you after I return to my room."

"Okay, Phil. One more question."

"What is it?'"

"What do you feel is the key piece of evidence that proves your innocence?"

"The fact that Jane had only one drink with me at the Small Planet restaurant which was made by the establishment and there were no available witnesses from that restaurant to come forward and say that she was incapacitated when we left. She came on to me in the car. Jane let back her seat and said, 'Let me teach you how to kiss.' And after our sexual encounter, she told me to drop her off at another bar, where she reportedly continued drinking. She told the police that she visited two bars before actually coming to the police station to file charges."

"She admitted this?"

"In her statement to the police, she admitted to attending two bars after we parted ways."

"And she continued to drink?"

"Yes, there were witnesses that saw her there drinking. That's why her blood alcohol level was so high by the time she made it to the police station. Our expert witness testified that there was no possible way she could have been legally intoxicated based on the level of alcohol contained in one Long Island iced tea."

"So the truth is that she wasn't intoxicated when she was with you."

"That's the truth."

"What would be her motive to lie?"

"Money?"

"You believe that someone paid her to do it?"

"Yes, I do."

"Who?"

"Grady Peninger, the former Michigan State Wrestling coach, and Dan Severn, my former assistant coach."

"Well, Phil, that's quite a theory. I will follow up with you on a later date because I think we've overstayed our welcome."

I felt tightness in my wrists as Deputy Sellik carted me out. They didn't want me to go any further. They didn't want me to tell my story. On my way down the aisles, I thought about my family; I imagined the face of my beautiful wife, Peggy, and when I closed my eyes, I could see freedom. I could see the light at the end of the tunnel, and it was the brightest light I had ever seen. I opened my eyes realizing that I would be out soon, and maybe then I could expose the truth. Peggy was coming to see me this evening at six o'clock, and it was four o'clock. I spent the next two hours by myself staring at the wall. It felt like an eternity waiting for Sellik to call me out.

"Your wife's here to see you," he said, and for the first time, his voice sounded like music to my ears.

For a moment, I felt exalted; for a moment, I forgot my woes.

Peggy stuck out like a sore thumb while nervously waiting for me in the visitation area. Her hair was vibrant. Her blond curls were bouncing about the shoulders of her black turtleneck, and she was wearing a red skirt and black clogs. We touched hands against the glass. I could hear my heart beating in my chest as we stood there for a while, looking into each other's eyes, smiling.

We moved our lips to the glass and closed our eyes.

"Sit down, my love," I said, taking a seat on the chair.

"I talked to David, and he wouldn't hand over the entered data that I needed for my dissertation. So he's trying to blame everyone else because he fucked up."

"Don't worry about it, Peg. It's about us right now. Words can't even describe how much I've missed you."

"It's been a nightmare, Phil. I just can't wait to get back to our lives."

"We're going to get through this. So don't lose hope."

"Let's leave it all behind."

"Believe me, Peg. I wish that I could. I wish that I could just go back."

"After you get out of here, let's leave this place in the past."

"I need to fight this."

"We've fought hard enough. We can't put the kids through this anymore. It's embarrassing to them, and they want to just forget about this fiasco. We can leave this nightmare in Lansing. That's why we moved to get away from this. We're living in Arizona now, and no one cares about all this there. So let's go where no one knows us and start over."

"We still have a chance to win if we don't give up."

"Let it go, Phil. It's too hard on the kids. They deserve to start with a clean slate."

"Okay, Peg. I will let it go, for now."

"Thanks, honey. You're almost out of here. I'm still so proud of you."

"Thanks, Peg. That means a lot to me."

"I love you, Phil. I will come to visit you tomorrow."

"Love you too, babe. I will be counting the hours until we meet again," I said, standing and moving toward her.

Our lips again touched the glass, and for a moment, when I closed my eyes, I could almost feel her. Deputy Sellik had to pull me out of the room because I didn't want to leave. My feet were weightless as I rushed through the halls on our way back to the dorm. When I got back to my cell, Elder Bonner was waiting for me.

"I just wanted to remind you never to lose hope, Phil," he said, half smiling.

"I sure won't," I assured him while we shook hands.

March 9, 1993

Sellik is on, and before heading into the gym, I felt someone touching my shoulder. I turned around to find *G* standing before me.

"Parker, you suck at basketball. Why don't you turn around and walk the other way?" he grunted, folding his arms over his chest.

"I was seven to one in the last two weeks while you're zero to one."

"Parker, all you do is sweat, get cold, and then freeze out there on the court."

"You ain't nothing but a druggie. I think you'd better move out of the way before I have to teach you a lesson."

Jasper then stepped between us.

"Ignore him, Coach. He doesn't know anything. He's just trying to get you riled up," Jasper said, pushing *G* back.

"If it went down, that punk would get hurt just as quickly as he could mouth my name," I lamented, gritting my teeth.

I was raging at this point and was about to snap. But I was tired of letting these chumps slide. Finally, when I got to the gym, the tension had subsided, and everyone was getting along. We won three games straight that day, and after recreation, Sellik stopped me in the hall.

"Peggy's here to see you," he said in a low tone. There was a trace of sympathy in his countenance.

"She's early," I replied.

"Well, that's better than her being late," he said, walking me to the visitation area.

Peggy was watching me from the other side of the glass, looking stunning. She was just as beautiful to me at that moment as she was the day we met.

"What's wrong?" I asked, pressing the phone against my ear.

"David's trying to sabotage me. He needs to release my paperwork so that I can finish my dissertation."

"He's a snake. Just keep pressing him, and sooner or later, he will give in."

"I don't know why he's trying to blame me for what happened to his career. I didn't have anything to do with his decision to start an affair with one of his clients. That's unethical behavior, and he knows it."

"I know. David's gone plum crazy. Just get your documents and then be through with him."

"That's what I'm going to do."

"You're the greatest woman in the world, and I'm so lucky that you're my wife. Nothing will ever come between us. Thank you for supporting me. You're my strength."

"I love you, Phil. There was a time when I didn't think you'd make it out of here. But I now know that you're going to walk out of these doors a better man."

"I've been to the desert, and I'm going to come out with a new sense of wisdom."

"I'm going to the University Club tonight to meet my friend Etta for dinner."

"Did you miss Michigan at all, Peg?"

"I only miss you."

"The next time we meet, it will be on the outside."

"I will be counting away the days."

"I love you, Peg."

"I love you more than anything," she whispered.

Her piercing blue eyes were tearing as we pressed our lips to the glass one more time. She looked radiant in that long flowing flowery dress, red lipstick, and those red high heels. Peggy was my rock; she was my light. I watched her leave the visitation area, and for a moment, I imagined myself breaking the glass with my fists. Oh, how I longed to hold her in my arms again. She was indeed my wild rose, and I truly loved her with all of my heart.

CHAPTER 15

Coming Home

March 10, 1993

I was soaking with sweat after working out in my cell. Today feels colder than the other days, and I remain optimistic despite it all. *G* got up for breakfast but stayed in at lunchtime. He seems to be hurting mentally and emotionally. This place affects people, and even the strongest tend to break down at one point or the other. I overheard him trying to convince the deputies that sports programming dominated his television time, but no one listened to his rants. We watched the NCAA Final Four basketball tournament all day. California upset Duke, and Western Kentucky beat Seton Hall. Both games went down to the wire. Bouee and Jasper gave me the thumbs up signal on my way back to my cell. After dinner, Jasper continued to scold Deputy Sellik with cold stares and threatening postures. I nudged him in the process. I'm not too fond of Sellik, and he knows it; but he was putting us both in grave danger this time. I spent the whole evening reading over my court transcripts. As I was reading, my mind began to drift far beyond the confines of the Ingham County Correctional Facility.

Through the words, I went back in time to the Lansing Fifty-Fifth District Court. I found myself moving through the fog of the empty courthouse until I reached room 5C. I then floated through the public doors of the court-room, interrupting my preliminary hearing. It was the *People v. Phil Parker,* and there wasn't an empty seat available on either side of the gal-lery. Judge Thomas Brown was sitting behind the bench rubbing his tired eyes as prosecutor Linda Berryman finished up her opening statement. I looked to the defender's table and could see the back of my head. John Frawley traversed the bench while carefully straying outside of *the well.* Frawley was running his fingers across his fluffy brown eyebrows. His thin lips were quivering. He was clean-shaven, and beads of sweat are roll-ing down the nape of his short, thick neck. His nose was red at the tip due to a recent bout with emphysema, and his light-brown hair was neatly cut around the ears. There was a cloud of dan-druff dusted about on the shoulder pads of his black sports coat, and his black slacks appeared to be at least two sizes too small.

"Mr. Frawley," said Judge Thomas.

"Thank you, Your Honor. We obviously, very strenuously oppose that motion. Mrs. Berryman has indicated that they have presented credible testimony. I very strenuously differ with her characterization of Jane Snow's testimony as being credible. First of all, we have no evidence on the record to indicate that there would have been any more alcohol in one drink that she clearly testified to have consumed. Her alcohol level was point one three at 1:50 a.m., the preceding hour would be the past hour that is believed," Mr. Frawley concluded, brushing past Stuart Dunnings on his way to the defense table.

Dunnings wore a double-breasted, light-blue sports coat with dark banker stripes and double-button barrel cuffs. I could hear the soles of his black square-toed shoes squeaking against the flooring as he moved to the bench, his gait exuding effortless swagger all the while.

Meanwhile, Dr. Todd Gross is patiently waiting on the witness stand. He is slightly damp around the collar of his English collared Royal Oxford. Gross is middle-aged and of French, Indian descent.

"You may proceed with your expert witness, Dr. Todd Gross," Judge Brown declared.

Just then, Gross folded his black-rimmed eyeglasses, placing them into the pocket of his baggy, tan slacks.

"Now, it could also mean a great deal more spread out over a longer period. Then from point one-nine over what? Four hours, that's the rate of metabolism assuming that no more was taken in and that would be expected," Dr. Gross explained.

"Doctor, given your experience, is it within a reasonable degree of medical certainty, as you understand it, that an individual who is suffering or losing consciousness as a result of alcohol would come in and out of consciousness?" Stuart asked, pacing the witness stand, thumbing his brown suspenders.

"Not unless they continued to drink," Dr. Gross replied.

"Doctor, within a reasonable degree of medical certainty, can you tell me whether or not the consumption of one and a half ounces of alcohol is sufficient enough to render a person helpless, physically and verbally, so that they would not be able to respond to a sexual assault?" Stuart continued, carefully shifting his attention from the judge to the witness stand.

"I don't think it would," Dr. Gross replied, clearing his throat.

"Why not?" Stuart asked.

"Pardon me?" Dr. Gross responded.

"Why not?" Dunnings asked once again.

"There's not enough alcohol in one and a half ounces of liquor to produce those kinds of changes," Dr. Gross concluded, sending a hush through the courtroom.

You could almost hear a pin drop while Stuart circled back toward the defense table.

"What do we have from the alleged victim by way of testimony as to her physical condition other than the fact that she simply stated she was physically helpless? We have her testimony as to seeing Phil Parker coming across the seat. We have her testifying as to the state of clothing of herself and Mr. Parker—the state of undress. We have her testifying that the incident of sexual intercourse, as she described, was brief. Now, if someone was physically helpless and unable to speak and unable to indicate a lack of consent, how do they know that? How would they possibly know all that? She was able to testify to those particulars. She was able to testify as to the events of the evening. We only have her bare assentation to indicate that she was physically helpless. It flies in the face of all the objective evidence that we have, of medical testimony from a qualified expert, who is schooled in the relationship of alcohol absorption. Who is schooled in treating alcoholics or people with other addictions, primarily alcohol, from experience at the Dimondale Center. His testimony is un-rebutted. It is the only medical testimony we have on record for you to consider in weighing whether or not her testimony is credible. The only testimony we have on the record regarding the number of drinks that Jane Snow consumed is her testimony, which is clearly one drink. She said, 'One drink.' Now it leads to the conclusion that she must have been drinking sometime or somewhere else within the hour before the point-one-three blood alcohol level was measured as at fifty a.m. on February the fifteenth. Regardless, even if it doesn't lead you to that conclusion, it must then mean that she lied about the number of drinks she had. Regardless, the testimony cannot be given any credibility. And I suggest to you that there is no possible way when you look at the whole matter when you consider the evidence submitted by the defense at this preliminary examination that this witness' testimony could be considered credible. It simply flies in the face of logic. It operates in the face of sworn statements, which, of course, is the only thing that you have to determine this case on. It flies in the face of objective scientific evidence. Clearly, she cannot be telling the truth. If she's not telling the truth, how can we justify binding this matter over on a matter of such magnitude and such enormous import and impact upon Phillip Parker? This is all you have to decide this case on. There's nothing to rebut, Dr. Gross. We have plenty to dispute in Jane Snow's testimony.

I respectfully request that you consider the credibility of this witness. I respectfully request that you dismiss this matter upon the lack of competency and credibility of the evidence that has been submitted against Phillip Parker," Stuart's voice suddenly faded into the darkness.

I then found myself sinking into the dimensions of my subconscious.

"You all right, Phil?" Jasper's voice brought me back to the present day.

I opened my eyes to a cold jail cell. I was sitting on the edge of the cot, looking down at the transcripts scattered on the floor.

"You looked like you were about to fall over," Jasper said, rolling from his side to his back on the upper cot.

"I was daydreaming, I guess," I replied, collecting the transcripts.

"Keep on fighting, Phil," Jasper grunted a few times before closing his eyes and surrendering to the night.

I carefully tucked the transcripts under my bed and then slid my tired body across the bottom bunk. For a while, I just laid there, staring into the darkness. Was it over? Or was this just the beginning? I asked myself these questions, knowing deep down that there was still hope for justice to prevail. There was still hope for my beautiful, loving family. I didn't want them to suffer anymore, but at the same time, I didn't want to let go of my chance to clear my name and my opportunity to be free again.

March 11, 1993

Tomorrow is my release date, and I'm feeling more robust than ever while walking through these all too familiar aisles. I was ecstatic about the idea of going back to my life on the outside. For some people, this is a revolving door, yet I knew in my heart that I would never be coming back to prison. Emotions were welling and, in essence, increasing my susceptibility to the scorn of my peers. I could feel them watching me in all directions. Their tired, weary eyes looked on, wondering what Coach Parker was going to do next. When I walked into the recreation room, Deputy Karn was operating the front of a blank television screen.

"What's wrong with the TV?" I asked before taking a seat somewhere in the front row.

By this time, Karn's round face is contorting, and his thin nostrils were flaring.

"We're not watching it right now, smart ass," he replied, glaring at me.

I was enraged by the arrogant, good-old-Mississippi-White-boy front that he was always putting on. Behind all his tough talk, I saw a scared little boy. He rolled back his broad, hefty shoulders and then tightened his back.

"Can you just turn it on?" I asked, looking directly in those quivering green eyes, and I saw nothing but pure fear staring back at me.

"Oh, you want to test me. I will show you. You're going to spend your last day in solitary confinement. That's where we like to put rabble rousers like you," he grunted, grabbing me by the arm, and within seconds, I was being rushed to the hole.

"Let's see if you think about the TV in here." Karn chuckled before slamming the cell door shut.

Again, I felt trapped in that dark, cold room without blankets or pillows. I could hear my teeth chattering as I sat on the floor, grabbing my knees for hours.

My legs were half asleep when Deputy Sellik finally broke the doors.

"Parker, it's time to go," he grunted, helping me to my feet.

I squinted in the light while stumbling into the aisles. My knees felt numb on my final stroll through these county jail halls.

"You can pick up your things in the lobby," he grunted, releasing my arm.

"I know," I replied.

I was half smiling while proudly stepping to the clerk's window. She was blond, middle-aged, and in an intractable mood. She kept scraping the tip of her sharp, pointy nose with her purple press-on nails.

"Phil Parker," she muttered in a low tone before turning her back and ducking out of view.

Minutes later, she was back, holding two plastic bags.

"Here," she said, handing me the bags containing a black short-sleeved polo, a pair of black slacks, black wing-tip dress shoes, and a black belt.

I quickly put on my clothes before following Sellik to the exit. I signed some paperwork at the door and then Deputy Sellik took me out of the exit gates where my friend, Judy Becker, was waiting, wearing a dark-blue dress. Her sandy-blond hair was flowing in the breeze.

"Phil, you look so thin," she said, grinning from ear to ear.

"The food's not so great in here," I replied, chuckling under my breath.

The wind was soothing to my skin as I walked through the breezy afternoon, feeling like I had a new lease on life. Judy led me to her red sedan, and before I got into the car, I took a moment to look back at the Ingham County Correctional Facility. I was ready to leave that desolate place behind, but still, I knew a part of me would linger behind those unforgiving walls; a part of me would remain tangled in the system, at least until I am exonerated. The only way for me to be genuinely free would be to tell the world my story—to expose the truth. The justice system had utterly failed me.

"You all right, Phil?" Judy asked, batting her long, dark eyelashes.

"I'm just happy to be able to go on with my life. I want my life back. It's time to pick up the pieces once broken by militia justice," I replied, getting into the car, and soon enough, we were on our way to redemption...

*****

Landon

The sound of whispering voices awakened me. My knees cracked as I jumped out of bed, yawning. I took a deep breath before opening the door and walking into the living room to find my parents holding each other.

"Is everything all right?" I asked before taking a seat on the couch.

"Mom's not feeling well," he replied.

224

His head hung low while he carefully led her into their bedroom. I closed my eyes, hoping that this was just a spell Mom was going through.

A few minutes later, Dad walked into the living room.

"What did you think of the diary?" he asked, taking a seat beside me.

"It brought the truth to the light."

"I kept everything, from transcripts to newspaper clippings. At the time, this case was a big deal," Dad said, setting the stack near the center of the coffee table.

"That's just what we needed—cold, hard evidence."

"Penned in those writings is a wealth of information, Landon."

"I was searching for the bridge to connect the present to the past, and I think I found it."

"My story is the bridge?"

"Yes, it is. I had to go back into the past and speak to the dreams to find clarity. Sometimes, I feel lost in between paper's lines."

"I understand you, son."

"The story will be my guide. I will let the words take me on a journey to the truth. My heart is leading my pen through this book."

"This book is all about heart, Landon."

"Heart?"

"It takes heart to become a champion."

"I know that's right."

"Martin Luther King Jr. was assassinated during my first year of college."

"Wow, tensions must have been high at Iowa State."

"They were out of control, especially after Chuck Jean hit an African American student over the head with a beer bottle."

"Chuck Jean, the All American?"

"I don't know if Jean was racist, but I know that he was meaner than a rabid coyote."

"Unbelievable."

"We were on the verge of civil war. Blacks were taking a stand against racism and injustice. It was the era of the Black Panthers and the Yuppies. We were the generation that evoked change."

"How did that situation play out in the Cyclone wrestling room?"

"We were on the verge of a race riot. The African American students were fighting the faculty tooth and nail. I remember the day when Nick came to me, asking for help."

"What did Coach Nichols want you to do?"

"He wanted me to tell the African American organizers that he wasn't racist."

"Did you?"

"No, I couldn't. I didn't want the Black students to label me an Uncle Tom. In hindsight, I regret the decision that I made. At the time, I was angry and militant. Nick was a good man though. He really cared."

"Coach Harold Nichols was a legend."

"I wanted to be a part of the movement. I was tired of reading about the tragedies. Names such as Emmet Till, Martin Luther King, and Malcolm X are among the lives that hate claimed."

"If you truly felt in your heart that Nick wasn't involved in the policies of hatred, then you should have spoken out. That's also being a part of the movement against injustice."

"I know. During those times, things weren't all that simple. Anyways, I'm glad that you read my writings."

"I am too. I always wondered what life was like for you behind bars."

"It was hard. I was in the desert, but I came out a better man. I'm going to bed, Landon."

"Good night, Pops," I said, looking at the stack of notebooks.

"Could this be the missing link?" I muttered, sifting through the pages.

Finally, after a few hours went by, I put the pen to the page, and, with each word, I took another step across the bridge.

EPILOGUE

◆◆◆◆◆◆

I *will never forget riding to the airport with my mom and sister to*
pick up my dad. It had been a year since I had seen him, and we
were eager to make up for the lost time. I couldn't wait to see my
dad again. Mom and Ann were in the front of our black '86 Honda
Accord while I was in the back, staring out of the window, looking into
the Arizona desert. On this day, I could barely feel the blazing heat that
had reached record temperatures. Mom turned on the radio, and we lis-
tened to smooth jazz the rest of the way there. We parked in the front lot,
and by the time I got out of the car, my feet were falling asleep on me. I
wondered if Dad's stay in jail had changed his physical appearance while
Mom quietly led us through sliding glass doors and up the escalator. She
was wearing her brand-new pink dress, and she had got a perm the day
before.

I was in a daze while we stood on the escalator. The wait was
finally over, and we felt triumphant over the thought of finally being
reunited with Dad. Our family would be whole again, and that alone
was therapeutic. We walked through the crowd looking for Phil Parker,
and suddenly we spotted him. It was Phil, the husband, father, and leg-
endary coach. Dad was looking thin, and his skin looked lighter than
usual. His face was bearded, and it looked like he had packed on at least
ten pounds of muscle. I'd never forgotten how tightly my parents held
each other at that moment. That's when I realized the rape charge hadn't
touched their conjugality. Their passion was a fire that burned eternally,
and through this hardship, their relationship had only gained momen-
tum. I watched him wrap Ann in his arms, wondering if this legend

would forever hang in a web of militia justice. I was proud of the way he stood and the way that white polo seemed to cling to his well-muscled frame. He then approached me with open arms. We hugged, and as we embraced, I finally felt safe again. I took a deep breath and then exhaled, letting all the tension release. These were the moments I would always cherish. Dad was back, and we would move on together. Like birds opening our wings, we soared out of the airport. There were smiles on our faces and a new sense of hope in our hearts. I was comforted by the reality that my family was back together again. I knew in my heart of hearts that one day, we would seek redemption; one day, we would correct the injustice of militia justice.

I took a deep breath before sliding my arms across the soft, leather couch.

"The last page," I mumbled while closing the final notebook of my father's diary. "It's time to tell the world about militia justice," I whispered, placing the journal on the top of the rest.

I took a few seconds to marvel at the neatly piled stack sitting on the coffee table, and I could only be thankful that those hard times were now a thing of the past. It was therapeutic for me to look back. At that moment, I realized that writing this story was healing my old wounds. The house was quiet until I heard the sound of brand-new tires grinding against the driveway. I could hear them talking outside but could not quite make out what they were saying. A few minutes later, the front door opened, and Dad wheeled Mom inside in a wheelchair.

"What happened to Mom?" I asked, shooting to my feet.

I wanted to hold her in my arms, but I kept my composure.

"She's not doing too well."

"Mom!" I cried out, fighting back the tears.

Mom's eyes were half closed.

"I'm so cold," she whispered.

She was shivering as my father wheeled her into her bedroom. My thoughts were racing as I found myself pacing the living room, trying to convince myself that she was going to recover. I kept telling myself that Mom would make it through this mess, yet with each passing day, her condition was only worsening. I waited for what seemed like an eternity before Dad finally came stumbling out of their room, looking defeated.

"What happened?" I asked, throwing my arms over the back of my head.

"Peggy and I just got back from the hospital, and we got some bad news today. Ann told me to make her go because she was slurring her words."

"She's all right. Don't overreact."

"She's not all right," Dad's voice was breaking, and by the sight of those tears snaking down his cheeks, I knew at once that there would be no turning back from here.

"What did they tell you?" I whispered, trying my best to suppress the pain.

"It went into Mom's brain," Dad replied in a low tone.

"No!" I growled, pounding my fist against the wall.

"Your mom's been fighting a long time, but it's time, son. It's just time."

"Don't say that. There must be something that we can do to save her. We can't just give up. She was doing fine. She was beating it."

"That's what we thought, but now it's taken over. The doctors say that there's nothing else that they can do. So we're going to put her on hospice."

"What about radiation treatment?"

"Ann claims that it won't help."

"We must try. How many tumors were in her brain?"

"More than fifty."

"This is devastating," I muttered, feeling empty inside.

I eased back on the couch with my shoulders slumped and my head hung low.

"You must stay strong, Landon," he said, reaching out and laying his hand on my left shoulder.

At that moment, I felt as if my whole world had come crashing down. I pulled my T-shirt over my face to cover the tears. I could hear Dad crying as I had never heard before.

Finally, I gathered my strength and stood to my feet.

"There's still hope. Mom's not gone yet," I mumbled, wiping away the tears.

"The doctors told Ann and me that there is nothing more that they can do."

"We must fight this!"

"Ann doesn't think we should try radiation therapy. We don't want to put Momma through that. She's already been through enough."

"We can't give up. We can't just put Momma in hospice. We can't just let this horrible disease ravage her body. But miracles can happen, and what we need is a miracle."

"Sometimes, it's just too late for miracles, Landon."

"It's not too late. As long as Mom is alive, it's not too late."

"I will talk to Ann about the issue tomorrow."

"You have to. She's my mother too, and I haven't given up yet. I want her to continue the treatment, and I think that's what she wants too."

"We'll try Landon. We'll do our best. Maybe you're right."

I turned and proceeded toward my parents' bedroom.

"Where are you going, Landon?"

"To talk to Mom."

"She's tired right now. Let her rest."

"I know, I won't be long," I muttered, dragging my feet on my way into the room.

I found Mom lying on the bed. I quietly crept to the queen-sized bed and then knelt beside her.

"I love you, Mother," I whispered, grabbing for her hand.

Her eyes opened, and there were swirling clouds of blue around her pupils. At that moment, I broke down.

"What's wrong, Landon?" she asked in a labored, muffled tone.

"I don't want to lose you."

"You're not going to lose me," she replied, squeezing my hand.

Dad then entered the room.

"She needs to rest right now, Landon," he said, dimming the lights.

"I love you, Mom," I said, rising to my full height.

"I love you too, Land," she replied, trying her best to smile.

Although her body and mind were failing, her soul was more durable than ever, and her heart was still holding on. I went stumbling out of the room, telling myself that everything was going to be all right. I tried to convince myself that Momma was going to recover. I needed hope to keep her strong, to keep her believing that she would pull through. I was the last one left of us that still believed in miracles. I couldn't stop the tears from falling on my way into the guest bedroom.

"C'mon, man," I said to myself before collapsing on the bed.

All was quiet in my parents' house when I opened my eyes and awakened to a living, breathing nightmare. Just the thought of losing Momma had been haunting us since before I could remember. I would often make comments about how miraculous it was that Momma had survived over forty life-threatening surgeries. Today, she was barely holding on, and there was nothing anyone could do to help her. I desperately tried to remain hopeful. I wouldn't let myself realize that we were going to lose her. She was our diamond in the rough; she was the rock of the family.

"Momma's going to make it," I kept telling myself until I found the strength to go back into my parents' room.

I opened the door, and Mom was lying on the bed with her body wrapped in thick white blankets. At this point, she was shivering uncontrollably.

"Mom, are you all right?" I muttered, rushing to her side.

I knelt down and gently took her hand. She awakened, and tiny embers were burning behind those almond-shaped, piercing blue eyes. I knew at once that she was going but dared not to believe it.

"I love you, Mom."

"I love you too, Land," she replied, trying her best to smile.

"Please hold on," I whispered while whimpering under my breath.

"Landon, I want you to tell your story."

"I will, Mom."

"And Landon, you tell it on the mountain," she was muttering now, and her eyes were closing.

I took her hand, and I could feel her strength failing. Dad entered the room, shaking his head.

"The hospice nurse is here," he announced.

His voice was low, and I could tell that he was fighting back the tears. I gathered my strength and stood to my full height, still holding Mom's hand.

"Let go, Landon. Just let go," Dad said, reaching out.

"I can't. I cannot give up on Mom. I can't give up on hope."

"Mom is suffering. Don't you want her to be free of the pain?"

"I don't want to lose her. I'm not ready to lose her."

"Mom is a fighter. She's trying to fight for us, but what about her? What about her pain?"

"She wants to be here with us."

"I know, Landon, but it's time, and there's nothing we can do about it. Come on, son. It's time," he said, throwing his arm over my shoulders.

I gently let go of her hand and then he led me out of the room. Sherry Eaton, from the Hopeful Hills hospice team, was waiting in the living room. She had attractive features, sandy blond hair, big brown eyes, and a warm smile.

"I'm sorry," she said in a low, airy tone.

I felt uncomfortable breaking down in front of a stranger, so I quickly gathered my composure.

"Be strong, Landon," Dad said, patting me on the back.

I went into the guest room and collapsed on the bed. About twenty minutes later, Dad entered the room.

"Landon, Mom's going," he said, looking decimated.

I followed him out of the room, and Ann was waiting for us in the living room. We cried for what seemed like an eternity.

"I need to say goodbye to her," I whispered, pushing past them.

I gathered my courage before turning the doorknob and entering the room to see my beloved mother one last time. She was suspended on a cot. Her eyes were closed, and her arms outstretched, and her feet were overlapping each other. The hospice nurse was in the corner, looking horrified at the sight of a woman fighting so hard to live.

"Will she wake up?" I asked.

"I don't think so," she replied.

Right then and there, I stopped caring what people thought of me. At that moment, I didn't care anymore what people said or how they might judge me. I thought about the trips to the Snake River. I thought about the nights spent listening to my mother's sweet voice singing lullabies or reading bedtime stories. I thought about the picnics with egg salad sandwiches. The times that we laughed and the times we cried. I thought about white Christmases, the snowmen, gingerbread, and seven-layer bars. I thought about her eyes and that one-of-a-kind smile that would melt my heart every time.

"Do you want me to leave you two alone so you can say goodbye?"

"Please," I replied, staring blankly ahead.

The tears were streaming down my cheeks. I almost couldn't bear to look down and see my mom like that. It was as if she was being crucified right in front of me, and there was nothing I could do about it. After the nurse left the room, I knelt beside my mother and laid my right hand on her feet. I could feel her toes quivering, and I knew at once that she was still fighting.

"Goodbye, Momma," I whispered before standing and leaving the room.

The next day at 11:30 a.m., my mother left the earth. Dad, Ann, and I made a pact to set everything aside that prevented us from truly loving each other before. We let go of our differences because we now realized collectively that Peggy Parker's memory could only live on through us, through love. Love is what Dr. Peggy Parker was all about, and love is what she wanted for us. She loved our enemies and those less fortunate than us. My mom loved the homeless guy out there freezing by the bus stop; and most, of all, she loved her family. She taught us to be a family. She taught us to let nothing break our circle. She taught us how to love unconditionally, and her love was divine. She made us believe in love and hope. It was she who showed us the way to heaven on earth. Being her son was a taste of heaven, and she was and will always be our angel.

ABOUT THE AUTHOR

Since before he could remember, Landon Parker took part in the sport of wrestling. In high school, Parker enjoyed a thirty-nine-match winning streak and then competed as a junior college wrestler. Landon's indoctrination of Father Phil's "hip concept" was his recipe for success. The author's mission is to share with the world Phil Parker's brilliant coaching system and ultimately exonerate those falsely accused. Landon firmly believes that it's never too late to overturn the wrongs of the past; it's never too late for justice.

CPSIA information can be obtained
at www.ICGtesting.com
Printed in the USA
BVHW072345300123
657442BV00004B/104

9 781639 856732